PROPOSALS THAT WIN YOU THE JOB

Step-by-step guide to writing proposals
Product design process
Useful tools
Product design brief checklist
User profile checklist
Persona checklist
Glossary

1st Edition

PROPOSALS THAT WIN YOU THE JOB

Robert A Curedale
Copyright © January 2017 by Robert A. Curedale
All rights reserved
Published by Design Community College Inc.

The publisher and author accept no liability, regardless of legal basis. Designations used in this book may be trademarks whose use by third parties for their own purposes could violate the rights of the owners. The author and publisher have taken great care with all texts and illustrations in this book. The information contained within this book is strictly for educational purposes. If you wish to apply ideas contained in this book you are taking full responsibility for your actions. There are no representations or warranties, express or implied, about the completeness, accuracy, reliability, suitability or availability with respect to the information, products, services, or related graphics contained in this book for any purpose. Any use of this information is at your own risk. The author has made every effort to ensure the accuracy of the information within this book was correct at time of publication. The publisher and author do not assume and hereby disclaims any liability to any party for any loss, damage, or disruption caused by errors or omissions, whether such errors or omissions result from accident, negligence, or any other cause.

All rights reserved. No part of this publication may be reproduced, distributed, or transmitted in any form or by any means, including photocopying, recording, or other electronic or mechanical methods, without the prior written permission of the publisher, except in the case of brief quotations embodied in critical reviews and certain other noncommercial uses permitted by copyright law. For permission requests, write to the publisher, addressed
"Attention: Permissions Coordinator," at the address below.

Design Community College Inc.
PO Box 1153
Topanga CA 90290 USA
info@dcc-edu.org
Designed and illustrated by Robert Curedale
ISBN-1-940805-33-3
ISBN-978-1-940805-33-7

PROPOSALS THAT WIN YOU THE JOB

Step-by-step guide to writing proposals
Product design process
Product design brief checklist
Business checklist
User profile checklist
Persona checklist

Robert Curedale

Published by Design Community College Inc.
Los Angeles https://dcc-edu.org

CONTENTS

01	WRITING A PROPOSAL	01
02	THE DESIGN PROCESS	41
03	FORWARD PROPOSAL SECTIONS	71
04	DESIGN PHASE DEFINITION	99
05	END PROPOSAL SECTIONS	133
06	PAYMENT	167
07	USEFUL TOOLS	201
08	USER PROFILE CHECKLIST	245
09	PERSONA CHECKLIST	251
10	PRODUCT BRIEFING CHECKLIST	258
11	BUSINESS MODEL CHECKLIST	279
12	GLOSSARY	288
	INDEX	294
	ONLINE COURSES BOOKS IN THIS SERIES	307
	ABOUT THE AUTHOR	315

INTRODUCTION

When I started design consulting I did not know how to write a proposal. My design school educaction did not cover the subject. Over several years my business grew and I employed more and more designers. Decades later I was working in very large design firms with hundreds of employees managing very large projects. Along the way I learrned how to write successful proposals. I created this book as a resource for designers to fill a gap i availble information. Design companies rarely divulge details of their proposal writing. There are few authentic sources of information.

The most important tool for every designer after their portfolio is a design proposal. Your proposal determines whether you do design work. After you have delivered your pitch to your client and your client has requested a written proposal how do you go about it? The proposal should show your prospective client that you understand their needs, and are thinking long-term to establish a strong relationship. A strong proposal is a well-organized plan. It establishes the scope of work for a project. Your proposal must convince your client that you're the best fit for the job. This book explains how to make the strongest possible argument for why you're the best candidate to win the job.

Proposals cause anxiety for many designers. If you haven't done it before it can be a daunting task. Little is published that is useful for working designers. One of the most difficult areas to find useful information is the activity of preparing a client project proposal. When designers first start consulting work learning to write successful proposals is one of the obstacles that they must conquer in order to earn their living in design practice. It is an area that is often not covered in design education.

In this book is the time and materials model which is the most common model used in industrial design and a model used to varying extents in most disciplines of design. A proposal with terms helps create certainty about the agreement and avoid mismatched expectations. Proposals are necessary to get paid. A proposal should be built on a solid foundation of a good brief. I have included some questions that you should ask or consider when a brief is being prepared. Design projects often involve changes of direction and rework. If the client needs to change their brief during a project this is best managed by a change order. Never provide design solutions in proposals.

While a template is useful each proposal is always different. Your proposal should read like a document written expressly for each client. Over the years, I have written thousands of proposals and learned why some win and some lose. I have that you will find this material useful and help you deliver great design work.

AND BY THE WAY, EVERYTHING IN LIFE IS WRITABLE ABOUT IF YOU HAVE THE OUTGOING GUTS TO DO IT, AND THE IMAGINATION TO IMPROVISE. THE WORST ENEMY IS SELF-DOUBT

SYLVIA PLATH
American poet, novelist, and short story writer

01
WRITING A PROPOSAL

WHY WRITE PROPOSALS?

PROPOSALS ARE ESSENTIAL.
Having a written document ensures that all parties involved are on the same page and completely clear on exactly what will be delivered and how it will be delivered.

The more complex a project is the more valuable your proposal will be.

1. Having a written document ensures that all parties involved are on the same page and completely clear on exactly what will be delivered and how it will be delivered.
2. A proposal helps avoid mismatched expectations.
3. A proposal helps create certainty about an agreement.
4. A proposal helps you cover all the important matters and not overlook things.
5. A proposal helps reduce risk.
6. A proposal helps enforce the agreement and helps you get paid

Provide cost and deliverable information that's as complete as possible, based on the information you have. Propose a detailed time-line for the work. If you typically quote per project, outline everything that's included in the estimate, even if it seems insignificant. And set a time limit for the client to accept the proposal. Say that it is valid for 30 days. This will encourage the client to act, or at least express interest by asking for an extension.

While a template is useful each proposal is usually different.

You proposal should read like a document written expressly for them. Customize it for each client. A well thought out design brief is essential for a successful design outcome. It dramatically reduces the amount or rework necessary during a design project. The design brief is an important stage of the design process. One of the most critical areas is the definition of whom you are designing for, your customer. We have included a user profile checklist to help define your end user.

Creating a design brief is best done with a cross-disciplinary group representing the different functional areas of an organization including design, engineering, business management, sales and marketing. It is the designer's responsibility to have all the information necessary to write an accurate design proposal for the project.

We have created this these checklists to help you focus on what is important. Take the list to your initial meeting with your clients. Review the information as you work on the project and if the brief changes create a change order to cover the necessary additional work. Your contact may not be the decision-maker

Factors that affect the selection of a designer. The order will depend on the particular context

- Price
- Availability
- Speed
- Convenience
- Dependability
- Personalization
- Quality
- Reputation
- Risk

THE PROCESS OF WRITING A PROPOSAL

Before writing a proposal a designer often needs to do a lot of work identifying prospective clients, then marketing and pitching to them.

This process will determine whether a client works with you or explores more options.

In general, the process of drafting, negotiating and finalizing an agreement with a client will follow this sequence of activities:

Think about your creative process. Write down the ideal sequence of activities —phases, steps and milestones — that allows you to produce your best work. If you are active in more than one practice area, you may have several variations. Your own creative process should be the framework that you use for planning and managing projects.

A proposal is a detailed project document that defines the scope of work, the process, the schedule, and the total price (usually in the form of a fixed fee). It is a discussion document where the designer puts forward a recommended course of action for the client to consider. Many proposals go through several rounds of changes and negotiations before they are finalized. Some negotiations with the client may relate to project specifications while other discussions might focus on the legal terms and conditions. The final goal is to have one comprehensive document that, when accompanied by an appropriate set of terms and conditions and signed by both parties, serves as your agreement for the project.

CALCULATE A REALISTIC STANDARD HOURLY RATE.
Rates vary from firm to firm based on the amount of overhead being carried, the number of hours available to devote to client projects and the target profit margin included in the calculation.

REVIEW THE BRIEFING QUESTIONS
In chapter ten you will find a list of briefing questions. Review the questions as a starting point for thinking about the information atht you will need to write the proposal.

GATHER AS MUCH INFORMATION AS POSSIBLE ON THE POTENTIAL PROJECT.
If the client has provided you with an Request for a proposal as a written document review that document. carefully.. Create a list of the questions that you need to ask the client.

MEET YOUR CLIENT FOR THE DESIGN BRIEF
Discuss the questions with your client that are relevant to your project. Be thorough. A gap in your knowledge in the brief may cost you or your client a great deal later on by having to redo work based on incorrect of too little information.Poor preparation at this stage can use up all your profit on a design project. Leave the list of questions with your cleint and ask them to gather the information that they were not able to give you and email it to you by a certain date perhaps a couple of days after the meeting.

Creating a design brief is best done with a cross-disciplinary group representing the different functional areas of an organization including design, engineering, business management, sales and marketing. It is the designer's responsibility to have all the information necessary to write an accurate design proposal for the project.

The proposal should be no longer than necessary to communicate what you need to communicate to the client in order for them to work with you

A well thought out design brief reduces the amount or rework necessary during a design project. The design brief is an important stage of the design process.

ASK YOUR CLIENT FOR THEIR BUDGET
I spend between two hours and two days preparing a proposal ranging in size between five pages and twenty-five pages. If you charge $150 per hour the investment in time as billable hours is between $300 and $3000 I usually give my clients a range or ballpark estimate verbally before writing a proposal. This eliminates the clients who do not have the resources to hire a designer. Clients understandably often are reluctant to diclose their budget. Later in this chater are some recommendations for how you can uncover your client's resources which can save you a lot of time and cost if they are not adequate to hire you.

Do some additional research before writing your proposal.
1. Define the problem or unmet need that your design will address. How can you meet this need with your design better than anyone else?
2. Research competitive brands and products. Which ones are the best? Where are there gaps in the market?
3. Call vendors and suppliers. Ask then about the competitors and about your client.
4. Define your audience. Who are they? Where do they live? What age range are they? What gender are they? What is their income and education and any other

Writing a proposal

relevant factors that help define the segment that you are designing for.
5. Do a credit check on your prospective client to ensure that they do not have a history of court actions for non-payment or fraud. There are many companies such as Dunn and Bradstreet that offer these services for a small fee.
6. Do some research about the person who will be approving the proposal and the person who you are presenting it to. I uses resources such as the LinkedIn profile to understad something about their personal backgrounds.

BEGIN DRAFTING THE PROPOSAL.
Write down all of the information that your client gives you and include it in your proposal so the client will review it before signing the authorization to proceed.This is important because then you are able to use change orders to manage and cahrge for any deviations from the original brief.

Prepare a spreadsheet of budget hours and costs for each stage. This ballpark number should be based on
1. The scope of work required
2. Your own design process
3. The size of the team that will be needed
4. Estimated number hours for each team

Not every proposal wins a contract. Monitor the success rate. If you are not successful follow up and ask your client why. The difference between a project's success and its failure is in the details. Relationships fail when each side has different expectations of the relationship

member and each stage
5. Committment To Other Clients
6. Estimated outside purchases including a standard markup
7. Define the design package in detail
8. Focus on customer's perspective
9. Recognize that designer's perspective is different from the customer's perspective
10. Define quality for tangible and intangibles elements
11. Reduce perceived risk

Adjust the totals to reflect market conditions and the value of the work to the client.

Create a schedule as a Gantt chart that shows blocks of time and indicates project activities that can happen concurrently. It is best to avoid showing specific start dates, approval dates or completion deadlines as they will change. Show each stage as a duration in days or weeks from the start.

Your proposal will contain some or all of the following sections:

LEADING SECTIONS
1. Cover Letter
2. Cover page
3. Table of contents
4. Executive summary
5. Current situation
6. Project goals & objectives
7. Competition
8. Audience
9. Strategy
10. Process

PHASE DESCRIPTIONS
11. Project individual phase descriptions

END SECTIONS
12. Fees & Reimbursements
13. Billing
14. Schedule
15. Terms & conditions
16. Conclusion
17. Next steps
18. Company overview
19. Project team
20. Clients
21. Awards

Make your proposal present the strongest possible argument for why you're the best candidate for the project. You should give as much definition to the project as pooossible but shorter proposals tend to be most successful. Limit your proposal to five pages if possible for a smaller project by covering each section in one or two paragraphs.
This will not be possible for larger projects. Customize it for each client. Clearly define your end user and how you will understand what is important to them.

We have created this these checklists to help you focus on what is important. Take the list to your initial meeting with your clients. Review the information as you work on the project and if the brief changes create a change order to cover the necessary additional work. Your contact may not be the decision-maker

FILE FORMATS
Proposals are often written using MS word .doc format. Pdf file format is the most common file format supplied to a client.

MAKE SURE YOU'RE ACCESSIBLE.
Include multiple methods for the client to contact you. The client should have your email address and a phone number, but also consider including your cell number, text or other ways to reach you.

ESTABLISH A TRACK RECORD
Before you start writing a proposal you must position yourself within your field of expertise to be known to the client known as someone who is both knowledgeable and credible and who can deliver value.
1. Are you dependable?
2. What relevant experience do you have?
3. Do you have sufficient resources to do the work including equipment and people?

CLEARLY DEFINE THE SCOPE OF WORK
Clearly and precisely define everything connected to your payment.
1. Is there an upfront payment?
2. Will you be paid at delivery, according to set milestones, or for your time?
3. Will there be a project cancellation fee?
4. Will there be a fee ffor late payment?
5. Are expenses included in your estimate?
6. What will be the method of payment?

Time and materials, royalties, retainer or other method.

DEFINE WHO WILL OWN YOUR WORK
1. Who can use your design? When, where, and how can they use your design?
2. Is the license exclusive? Can the work be sold to other clients?
3. Can your client modify the design?

FOLLOW UP QUESTIONS IF YOU DO NOT HEAR BACK WITHIN ONE WEEK
1. Are there any updates for us?
2. Are you free to chat this week Peter?
3. Let me know what makes sense as a next step, if any?
4. I'm writing to follow up on our last conversation. My boss asked me for an update on your account. I told him I didn't have one.
5. Have you given any additional thought to my proposal? I'd be happy to do a quick review of it on the phone and answer any pending questions.
6. I'm writing to follow up on my email. I didn't hear back from anyone on the team. If it makes sense to talk, let me know how your calendar looks. If not, who is the appropriate person for me to talk to?
7. Just let me know if you have any questions or would like to have a more in-depth conversation. I'm here whenever you need me.
8. We are in the process of closing files for the month. Typically when I haven't heard back from someone it means they're either really busy or aren't interested. If you aren't interested, do I have your permission to close your file? If you're still interested, what do you recommend as a next step? Thanks for your help.

hubspot.com

HOURLY RATE

CALCULATE A REALISTIC HOURLY RATE

How many billable hours can you expect to work in a year? The average solo designer spends about 50 percent of their time marketing, selling administering, learning, re-doing client work, doing client work that can't be billed, and more. All of those are hours that don't earn dollars. If you're a solo designer working 1920 hours a year, it's likely you're working around 1000 billable hours. Set up a time sheet and record the number of hours you work and where the time is going. You need also to take into account expenses

Rates vary from firm to firm based on the amount of overhead being carried, the number of hours available to devote to client projects and the target profit margin included in the calculation.

THE DAILY OR HOURLY RATE DEPENDS ON:

- Your experience
- Your unique value proposition
- Your geographic location
- How long the work is for: if the work is for a longer period then the daily rate may go down
- When the work is: for night or weekend work you can ask more
- The market rate
- Your ability to negotiate

> "Confidence in pricing is really about a state of mind. Positioning yourself as the expert is the catalyst that sees you behaving as one.
>
> Once you start behaving as the expert you start thinking like one and then – well, then you start to price like one!"
>
> *Amanda Jesnoewski, Five tips for charging what you're worth*

HOW DO I CALCULATE MY FREELANCE DESIGN RATE?

- Identify your annual expenditure. Don't forget to include your rent, phone, travel, insurance, equipment needs, meeting space, materials, and marketing.
- How many clients do you get each month on average?
- How many hours each week do you spend marketing?
- How many hours each month do you spend writing proposals and presenting them to prospective clients?
- Identify the equipment and software that you need to purchase.
- Then identify how much you would need as a salary.
- Include tax.
- Calculate how many hours you can invoice
- Depending on experience non-billable time may be 40% to 60% of total work time.
- 48 weeks x 40hours x 50% = 960 hours p.a.
- For long-term fixed contracts decrease your hourly rate in return for a more steady stream of billable hours.
- Longer term contracts provide stability and increase your percentage of billable hours.
- Never work without a proposal and signed contract
- Decide on your margin for profit.
- A profit margin, however small, has to be anticipated, otherwise your business will not grow.

When you start to charge what you are worth, you'll find something incredible happens: you'll attract better clients, clients who see the value in what you provide and are more than happy to pay your bills.

Amanda Jesnoewski, Five tips for charging what you're worth

COMBINING FONTS

Text Font \ Heading Font	Avant Garde Gothic	Bauhaus	Bembo	Bodoni	Bookman	Caslon	Century	Cheltenham	Franklin Gothic	Futura	Garamond	Gill Sans	Helvetica	Kabel	Korina	Quorum	Optima	Palantino	Souvenir	Times New Roman	Univers	Zapf Book	Comic Sans

■ Combine

▨ Combine with care

☐ Never combine

TYPOGRAPHY & LAYOUT

TYPOGRAPHY
Your business documents are part of your portfolio. They should communicate your design skills. Make sure it looks good and communicates well.

A proposal is a system of visual communication. using fonts, text placement, images, color, white space and layout working together to communicate that you can be a skilled designer.

The elements :
1. Should speak one design language
2. Should communicate consistently
3. Should be visually consistent with your resume, business card, letter of introduction and personal brand.
4. Should not be visually confusing
5. Should have a visual hierarchy to support your communication strategy
6. Contrast should support your communication strategy.

DO NOT USE TOO MANY FONTS
Use at least two different fonts; one for headings and one for body content. Do not use more than three fonts. Too many fonts can distract from the content of your proposal.

FONT STYLES
Mixing serif and sans serif can add interest and readability. Use a readable font, Sans-serif for titles and a light weight serif for body text. Use no more than three fonts.

Use consistent fonts and font sizes throughout your proposal. Use the same fonts in your resume, cover letter, business card and portfolio.

Take care with everything that you place on the page. Have a design strategy and follow the strategy consistently. Don't use too many fonts. The most important information should be bolder or larger on the page. Space paragraph text with more leading than the default. 10 point font could have 16 point leading.

COMBINING FONTS

Don't use a font size smaller than ten point. Use a minimum font size 10 to 12 pt. Use consistent font sizes. The person interviewing you may have poor vision. Use the sizes of the fonts to support the communication visual hierarchy. Bigger text attracts attention first. Larger text is more important than the smaller text.

PAIRING FONTS
Here are some guidelines for pairing fonts.
1. Don't use too many fonts.
2. Choose complementary fonts
3. Use a sans-serif for the headline. Use a serif font for the byline/body text.
4. Establish a visual hierarchy.
5. Create contrast
6. Avoid pairing fonts that are too similar
7. Use different weights of fonts from the same family
8. Mix fonts from the same historical period
9. Consider context
10. Don't mix different moods

Multiple fonts work best together when they have similar proportion and scale. Pair fonts, one for the titles and the other one for the text. Georgia and Verdana have similar shapes, even though one is serif and one is sans serif. Times New Roman and Arial Narrow are also harmonious fonts. A common approach which can work well is to use one sans serif for the headline and a serif for the body copy.

DECORATIVE FONTS
You should avoid fonts that have decorative shapes, ornaments such as script fonts. Comic fonts are often used by designers with poor graphic skills and are best avoided unless you are a cartoonist.

FONT WEIGHT
Choose a typeface that has a number of variations in weight and style so that you can provide emphasis for text elements. Bold

GOOD FONTS FOR PROPOSALS

Gill Sans
The quick brown fox jumps over the lazy dog

Helvetica
The quick brown fox jumps over the lazy

Arial
The quick brown fox jumps over the lazy dog

Futura
The quick brown fox jumps over the lazy

Bodoni
The quick brown fox jumps over the lazy dog

Clarendon
The quick brown fox jumps over the lazy

Verdana
The quick brown fox jumps over the lazy

BAD FONTS FOR PROPOSALS

Avoid decorative fonts. In the hands of an inexperienced designer they can lose you the job.

COMIC SANS
THE QUICK BROWN FOX JUMPS OVER THE LAZY DOG

Ferro Rosso
The quick brown fox jumps over the lazy dog

Nately
The quick brown fox jumps over the lazy dog

ROSEWOOD
THE QUICK BROWN FOX JUMPS OVER THE LAZY DOG

BRUSH SCRIPT
The quick brown fox jumps over the lazy dog

DISTANT GALAXY
THE QUICK BROWN FOX JUMPS OVER THE

Medieval Queen
The quick brown fox jumps over the lazy

weights provide options for creating emphasis and defining hierarchy. Use bold type sparingly to avoid distraction.

LEGIBILITY
1. Text set in lower case is more legible than text set all in upper case or capitals.
2. Regular upright type Roman type is more legible than italic type.
3. Greater contrast, helps legibility.
4. Positive images black on white are easier to read than negative or reversed white on black.

CONTRAST
For best readabliity allow adequate contrast between the text and background. Don't use thin text on a dark background. Do not use light text on a light background or dark text on a dark background or any text that is close in contrast level to the background.

IMAGES
1. All images should have a purpose related to what you need to communicate. Do not use images just to make the document look attractive.
2. Make sure that all images have suitable resolution and are not pixilated.
3. If using images of people to communicate professionalism, personality, and intellect use a large face with less of the body
4. If using images of people to communicate health, vigor, and sensuality include more of the body.
5. Do not use images that are pixilated or distorted in any way; your document will

lose immediate credibility.
6. Make sure all faces of people look toward the inside or spine of the document. Avoid having images of people looking off the page.
7. When using multiple photos in the same document, make sure that their photographic styles, including lighting, position, and colors are consistent.

REPETITION
Repeat the design elements such as the headings and text placement to create consistency. Too much consistency can make a document seem uncreative.

GROUPING
Place information near related information. Group headings with content. Make sure that image captions are clearly associated with the appropriate image.

ALIGNMENT
Every element is aligned with something else. Do not place any element arbitrarily. Every alignment should be precisely aligned.
Centre alignment is best avoided.

MARGINS & GUTTERS
Ensure all text and images have enough space between them to be readable.

PROPOSITIONAL DENSITY
Communicate more ideas in a page than visual elements.

Common mistakes

1. Use simple language
2. Avoid jargon
3. Don't try to force in too much content Less is more.
4. Consider the document navigation carefully
5. Design the portfolio for the audience not other designers.
6. Include a phone number and email on every page

COLOR

Use color to support your design communication strategy. Maintain consistency of palette and usage throughout.

1. Do not use too many colors.
2. Restrict use of color in the layout to three or four colors.
3. Use color to communicate messages
4. Red for vitality or
5. blue for trust and security.
6. Consider cultural responses to colors. Colors have different associations in different cultures.
7. Create strong contrast to ensure readability. Use harmonious color schemes: such as monochromatic, analogous, complementary, triadic, quadratic or split-complimentary color schemes.
8. Do not use complementary colors in close proximity as this will result in visual vibration and difficulty reading text.
9. The dominant colors in the images should be harmonious with color used elsewhere in the layout. Don't use too much black.
10. Be cautious about special-effect colors: metallic/reflective, luminescent, fluorescent or brilliant, glowing colors.

EFFECTS

Avoid drop shadows and gradients.

VISUAL HIERARCHY

Give visual cues to guide your audience through the most important information to the least important information.

TRUST YOUR INSTINCTS
Step back from the details and look at the big picture. If something doesn't look right or feel right to you, rework it.

ERNEST HEMINGWAY'S TOP 4 TIPS FOR SUCCESSFUL WRITING

Ernest Hemingway had a simple direct writing style that dispensed with unnecessary fat and got straight to the point.
These are Hemingway's rules:

1. Use short sentences.
    Hemingway was challenged to tell a story in 6 words.
    "For sale: baby shoes, never worn."
2. Use short first paragraphs.
3. Use vigorous English.
    Use strong, forceful, vital language that communicates passion, focus and intention. Use words that create vivid pictures in the mind of your reader that they can easily relate to
4. Be positive, not negative.
    Instead of saying "inexpensive," say "economical,"
    Instead of saying "painless," say "little discomfort"

PRICING STRATEGIES

Good pricing strategies are one of the most effective paths to a profitable business. Research shows that if a business raises its prices by just 1 per cent, its profits can increase by 11 per cent. Increasing price is often more effective than increasing selling volume for the average business in creating profit.

BEFORE YOU PRICE YOUR PROJECT
Do you know what your competitors are asking or getting for similar work? Do some practical market research. Does your estimate compare well with your competition's pricing? Ask your potential client for a budget during your very first meeting with them. My very rough estimate on a project like this will probably be somewhere between $15K and $30K. Does that sound reasonable to you?" This will validate the client to ensure that they have an understanding of the budget range of the project. Always show prices in proposals as estimates.

PRICE-BRACKETING
Lay out a pricing table with three options for your services and deliverables as opposed to just one option. If a client thinks that your initial cost is too high consider adjusting deliverables for a lower price.

BUNDLE PRICE
Offer a discount if buyers want more of your services at the same time, or if they book at the same time, to encourage them to buy more.

TWO-PART PRICING
This is like a sign-on fee. The customer pays you an upfront amount, which then gives them the right to a smaller ongoing hourly fee. Like Costco, but for design. A good model if you have a service that involves a high cost of set-up.

BEFORE YOU PRICE YOUR PROJECT

Do you know what your competitors are asking or getting for similar work? Do some practical market research. Does your estimate compare well with your competition's pricing? Ask your potential client for a budget during your very first meeting with them. My very rough estimate on a project like this will probably be somewhere between $15K and $30K. Does that sound reasonable to you?" This will validate the client to ensure that they have an understanding of the budget range of the project. Always show prices in proposals as estimates.

Inexperienced design consultants tend to undercharge for their services. They try to compete on price but underestimate how much a business will cost to run.

PRICE-BRACKETING

Lay out a pricing table with three options for your services and deliverables as opposed to just one option. If a client thinks that your initial cost is too high consider adjusting deliverables for a lower price.

BUNDLE PRICE

Offer a discount if buyers want more of your services at the same time, or if they book at the same time, to encourage them to buy more.

TWO-PART PRICING

This is like a sign-on fee. The customer pays you an upfront amount, which then gives them the right to a smaller ongoing hourly fee. Like Costco, but for design. A good model if you have a service that involves a high cost of set-up.

Discounting

Price is usually not the number one consideration when clients select a particular designer.

For every dollar a client spends on design they may spend ten dollars on tooling and setting up manufacture of a product and one hundred dollars setting up distribution, launching and promoting a product

Giving a discount doesn't work for creative businesses as it can make you look cheap, and creative products and services are rarely bought purely on their price.

Offer other incentives in quiet periods such as January.

PROJECT EVALUATIONS

Charge a fixed price to evaluate the project, and give them your recommendations.
A "Project Evaluation", is a detailed plan for the work that is to be done on a project, and explains how it will be done. An evaluation includes a paid research phase. It is commonly about 5% to 10% of the total design cost.
If a client is unwilling or unable to pay for a project evaluation, it can be an indicator that the project isn't a match.

COST PRICE

Do you know how much it actually cost you to produce your work, material costs, overhead and hourly cost? You need to know your 'break even point'. With this method the designer takes the greatest risk.

VALUE BASED PRICING

Value-based pricing is based on what your value creation is. How much value does your work add to your client's business? Many designers and makers underestimate the value they create for their clients.

PREMIUM PRICE

Your price tells a story. Where you want to position yourself, who your dream clients are, what your profile is, what the value is of your work. Are you able to charge more because you have more expertise, are more exclusive, your brand, your position in the market and your target audience?

INTERNATIONAL PRICE

Check out the local market, local prices and what your competitors charge locally, as different markets can differ. Check conversion rate trends.

BUNDLE PRICE

Offer a discount if buyers want more of your services at the same time, or if they book at the same time, to encourage them to buy more.

EMERGENCY PRICE

Will you have to work many many hours deep into the night to get the work delivered in time? Consider increasing your hourly rate to compensate for the added effort.

CAPPED PRICE

Give an upper limit to the project cost, which is somewhat higher than your estimated cost. You should make a provision for no variations to brief.

"I never charge 50% down and 50% upon completion. That's old school and when a client drags their feet on items, the final 50% won't arrive for many months later. My advice is to break the payments into equal monthly payments. People prefer subscription payments because it's a set budget. No surprises."

Source Sean Tepper

QUOTE BY VALUE

Stage	Value	Price
Website Design	$1,000	$1,000
Mobile Friendly	$2,000	$2,000
Contact Form	$1,000 *	$250
Payment Form	$1,500 *	$500
TOTAL	$5,500	$3,750

* This proposed solution is a website component that has already been developed for a company similar to your company. Because this component has proven to be effective for their website, we will use this same component for your website *Source Sean Tepper*

FIXED PROJECT BUDGET
Project has a total given price, which is often divided into different stages with according fees i.e. 30% deposit upfront, 50% creative stage, 20% delivery stage. This has risk for the design company as clients often add requirements during a project. Only work with a contract.

RETAINER
Consider offering a lower hourley rate for your customers if they were to have a monthly retainer for a longer term. This triggers the fear of loss in your client's minds. This works well for designer and client.

ALL-YOU-CAN-EAT
You set a higher price and your customer can then have as much work done as they wish in a time frame.

TWO-PART PRICING
This is like a sign-on fee. The customer pays you an upfront amount, which then gives them the right to a smaller ongoing hourly fee. Like Costco, but for design. A good model if you have a service that involves a high cost of set-up.

EXTRA FEATURES PRICE
If you are providing services you can think about different 'packages' that you offer at different price levels. The client can select the features to fit their budget.

WHY PROPOSALS FAIL

YOU DIDN'T BUILD RAPPORT.
Learn about their business, but learn about them as people. They don't have your necessary budget. Talk about budget honestly and openly, set expectations, and then deliver a proposal.

YOU DIDN'T TURN IT AROUND FAST ENOUGH.
Turn around proposals in seven calendar days or less from the initial meeting.

YOU TALKED TOO MUCH ABOUT COST AND NOT ENOUGH ABOUT VALUE.
If your proposals are focused only on the cost of your service or product and not the value of it, you're missing a big opportunity.

YOU DIDN'T TAKE A UNIQUE POSITION.
You will be in situations where you are one of multiple design companies asked to submit proposals for the same project. What is every other shop going to say? What are their unique angles going to be? And how can you differentiate yourselves?

UPSELL, INSTEAD OF STARTING WITH EVERYTHING, THEN REMOVING FEATURES.
Instead of starting at the lowest-cost option and adding on features, start at the highest-cost option and remove features. The result here is a shift in perception on the client end: their thinking goes from "These extra features cost more" to "I don't get these features with the Standard package." It's a simple form of loss aversion.

Not every proposal wins a contract. Monitor the success rate. If you are not successful follow up and ask your client why. The difference between a project's success and its failure is in the details. Business relationships tend to fail when each side has different expectations of the relationship

The most successful designers enjoy marketing and networking. People skills are important in freelance design. A great portfolio is not enough. Half of what influences a client to give you work is often whether the client likes you personally and wants to spend time working with you.

YOU TALKED TOO MUCH ABOUT WHAT YOU'LL DO, NOT HOW THE CLIENT WILL BENEFIT.
Instead of: "We will design you a camera with plastic parts." Instead, rewrite it to focus on how the client will benefit:"We will design you a camera that will be more profitable because it fills a gap in your product range."

You're letting the client know a tangible deliverable and a benefit associated with it. You gave up too soon. The purchasing cycle is a decision cycle, and dependent on the level of cost and risk involved, it varies greatly. Follow-up to your proposals. This may need to be done two or three times. Help answer questions and move the decision process along.

BEING TOO VAGUE WITH YOUR QUESTIONS.
Ask specific questions Instead of "Please let me know how I can help", say "What do you want to accomplish within the next 12 months?"

TALKING JARGON
Don't use technical jargon. Discuss the client's needs in terms you'd use with an outsider.

NOT LISTENING TO YOUR CLIENT'S GOALS.
Ask very specific questions. „What is the number one thing preventing you from accomplishing this?"

Writing a proposal

THE PROSPECT IS A SCAMMER
Always only start work with a contract. Beware of clients who ask for design concepts free with a proposal. Beware of clients who miss payments.

FREE PITCHING
Don't provide design solutions in proposals. If you do then the client does not need to hire you.

START WITH SOMETHING SMALL
If you are uncertain about a client start with a small project where your risk is low.
• Propose something that would be of little risk.
• Require a small commitment.
• Test to see if you and the client are a good fit for each other.
• Open up the door for a bigger projects.
• Afterwards get feedback from your client,
• Learn more about how you can best work with them.

DEADLINE FOR PROPOSAL SUBMISSION WAS NOT MET

GUIDELINES FOR PROPOSAL CONTENT WERE NOT FOLLOWED EXACTLY
Give the client as a minimum what they ask for.

PROPOSALS ARE HARD FOR THE CLIENT TO UNDERSTAND OR ACCESS
Keep jargon to a minimum and arrange the document in a logical way.

The budget was too high or the budget was too low.

You may not be selected because you appear to be quoting too low. I have worked on projects where we have obtained hundreds of quotations. When you solicit a large number of prices they appear to be in several clusters. The lowest cluster off prices indicates that the design company or vendor is inexperienced or not being honest. The client will select a lower price in the cluster that is realistic and also consider other factors such as experience with similar projects.

One of the most important factors is whether a client likes the person who is presenting and thinks that there is the basis of an ongoing relationship with whoever they will be working with.

Clients may have experienced design companies sending their senior partners to the initial meeting but placing interns on the project who lacked experience and oversight and so the project failed.

THE PROPOSED OFFERED NOTHING UNUSUAL, INTRIGUING.
Give them a proposal that leverages your unique skills and experience. If you are unable to do this then you must compete on price which is a poor strategy.

THE PROPOSAL WAS NOT COMPLETE
Describe all the stages and costs. Describe how the project will be managed and how success will be evaluated.

THE PROPOSAL SHOWED THAT THE DESIGNER DOES NOT UNDERSTAND THE SUBJECT MATTER
They will hire you only if you can show that you have expertise.

PROPOSAL APPEARED BEYOND THE CAPACITY OF THE DESIGNER
Show that you have the resources including sufficient people and equipment to complete the project successful.

COSTS APPEARED GREATER THAN THE BENEFITS

IT WAS UNCLEAR WHO WOULD BENEFIT
Quantify how the client will benefit

LESSONS LEARNED FROM PREVIOUS PROJECTS ARE NOT SHOWN
Show how your experience will benefit the client.

THE TASKS AND DELIVERABLES ARE TOO VAGUE
Be as precise as possible in quantifying what you will deliver.

THEY LACK SPECIFICS ON WHO WILL BE DOING THE ACTIVITIES
The client wants to know that the right people will be doing the work and not an under qualified person.

THE TIMETABLES FOR ACCOMPLISHING WORK ARE TOO OPTIMISTIC OR ILL DEFINED
Provide a detailed and realistic schedule

THE PROPOSAL IS TOO LONG
Keep it as short as possible.

THE PROPOSAL SHOWS AN INATTENTION TO DETAIL AND QUALITY OF WORK
Consider the proposal to be part of your portfolio

LITTLE VALUE OFFERED
Itemize and quantify the benefits

THE PROPOSAL CONFUSES FEATURES AND BENEFITS
What unmet customer and client needs are you addressing?

THE DESIGNER PROVIDES NO EVIDENCE TO BACK-UP AND SUPPORT WHAT THEY ARE OFFERING
Give relevant case studies and quantify the benefits

The biggest single cause off failure of design projects is lack of customer insight. 24% By one survey. Your proposal may make it evident that you have never met the real customer and the real customer has never met you. You may think that you know what the customer wants but are just guessing

The designer submits a generic proposal template. Do not resubmit and old proposal hoping that lightening will strike twice. Write each proposal specifically for the client, audience and project. I have found that it is good to have a template but I have found that it is always necessary to modify each proposal significantly from the template to win a project.

AFTER YOU SEND THE PROPOSAL

How long did it take you to write that proposal?
How long did it take for the client to get back to you?
Did you follow up?
Why did you win the project?
Why did you lose the project?

THE DESIGNER CONFUSES A CUSTOMER'S NEEDS AND WANTS
Sometimes the wants are more relevant for a project than the needs. This may be the case for example, with luxury products and services.

YOU ARE NOT SELLING THE BENEFITS
Define benefits to the client organization, the end user and the person that needs to sign off on the proposal as clearly as possible

THE PROPOSAL IS NOT WELL STRUCTURED.
Make the important information easy to find

THERE'S NO CALL TO ACTION.
You do not hear back from the client because they do not know what to do to initiate the project.

FAILURE
Businesses most often fail due to one or more of these four issues:
1. Inadequate sales (39%)
2. Competitive weaknesses (21%)
3. Excessive operating expenses (11%)
4. Uncollected receivables (9%).

WHAT CAN HELP YOUR PROPOSAL SUCCEED?

HAVE A TARGETED APPROACH
Know what your strengths are and define your unique value proposition in your proposal. Make your proposal unique. Don't try to be a generalist. A generalist competes on price.

FIND STRATEGIC PARTNERS
Find strategic alliance partners with whom you have a business and cultural compatibility. You will have a deeper pool of talent. Form winning teams.

ASSIGN ACCOUNTABILITY
Make sure every claim can be substantiated. Demonstrate who will be responsible for activities. Show that they are well-qualified.

FIND REAL DISCRIMINATOR(S)
The term "discriminator" describes something about your company that is truly unique.
The length of time that you have been in business or that you are ISO 9001 certified may not be a sufficient value proposition to win you a job.

BE A GOOD LISTENER
I have found that it is more successful to listen to them tell you what they need and provide that than to tell them how good you are.

UNDERSTAND YOUR CUSTOMER
When preparing proposals, focus on the customer's problems first, then your solution. What is it that keeps them up at night?

KEEP IT SHORT AS POSSIBLE
Research by the site Bidsketch over 25,000 client proposals found that proposals less than 5 pages long were 51 percent more likely to win than those that were longer.

DESIGN IS IN EVERYTHING WE MAKE, BUT IT'S ALSO BETWEEN THOSE THINGS. IT'S A MIX OF CRAFT, SCIENCE, STORYTELLING, PROPAGANDA, AND PHILOSOPHY

ERIK ADIGARD
a communication designer, multimedia artist and educator based in the San Francisco Bay Area

NEGOTIATING

f the proposal needs to change issue a new version number and write the date and the proposal and version numbers in the footer of each page. It is sometimes better to list negotiated changes to the terms and conditions on a separate sheet, called an addendum. The addendum must clearly describe exactly what is being changed and it must not create any contradictions or ambiguities.
Source AIGA

I present my proposal in person to the client always if that is possible. In my experience this increases the rate of aceptance by more than 50%. Clients often ask for modifications. It is common for clients to ask for a lower price. One of my clients said that he always asks for a lower price everytime he purchases something, even in a department store. Do not lower your hourly rate. Offer to reduce the deliverables for a lower price. It is natural psychology to avoid loss so clients usually do not want to reduce the deliverables. You can also change a deliveral to one which takes less time. For example a sketch rather than a computer rendering. Discuss the scope of work. Focus on the main objectives. Can portions of the project be scaled back? Are there components that can be later projects?

Most experienced designers ask for a deposit at the start of a project. Some designers apply the deposit to the first progress billing making it a pre-payment of phase 1. Others state that the deposit will be held until the end of project and applied to the final billing.

Take care to use the correct terms in your proposal. If you use the term Quote instead of estimate for example you may be committing yourself to unpaid work. There is a glossary with more terms at the end of this book.

ESTIMATE
An estimate is tentative and non-binding. It is a projection of the approximate costs that you anticipate on a project. The total is usually described as a rough "ballpark" figure or presented as a high/low range.

QUOTE
A quote is much more precise. It is a firm offer to perform specified services for a fixed price. For example, printing companies submit quotes based on the exact specifications provided to them by clients.

BID
This term is normally used when a client is seeking competitive prices from several different suppliers. Many corporations have strict guidelines for the competitive bidding process.

LETTER OF AGREEMENT
This is a written recap of items that have already been agreed to orally. It's a bad idea for any creative firm to begin a project solely on the basis of an oral agreement-always protect yourself by having a signed document. A letter of agreement is better than nothing, but it's smarter to submit a complete proposal.

NOT-TO-EXCEED
Watch for this term on documents that come to you from the client-particularly on corporate purchase orders. It indicates the maximum amount that can be paid for a project, including any taxes, shipping or other last-minute charges. You will not be able to bill for anything beyond this total without going through a lengthy re-authorization process.

BREAK-EVEN POINT
The output of the standard break-even analysis. The unit sales volumes or actual sales amounts that a company needs to equal its running expense rate and not lose or make money in a given month.

BUNDLING
The practice of marketing two or more product or service items in a single package with one price.### BUSINESS MISSION
A brief description of an organization's purpose with reference to its customers, products or services, markets, philosophy, and technology.

MISSION STATEMENT
A statement that captures an organization's purpose, customer orientation and business philosophy.

COMPETITIVE ANALYSIS
Assessing and analyzing the comparative strengths and weaknesses of competitors; may include their current and potential product and service development and marketing strategies.

NET PROFIT
The operating income less taxes and interest. The same as earnings, or net income.

POSITIONING
Orchestrating an organization's offering and image to occupy a unique and valued place in the customer's mind relative to competitive offerings. A product or service can be positioned on the basis of an attribute or benefit, use or application, user, class, price, or quality.

GROSS MARGIN
The difference between total sales revenue and total cost of goods sold (also called total cost of sales). This can also be expressed on a per unit basis, as the difference between unit selling price and unit cost of goods sold. Gross margin can be expressed in dollar or percentage terms.

Sources: AIGA and bplans.com

TROUBLE-SHOOTING CHECKLIST

1. Have you followed the guidelines in this guide and included all relevant sections?
2. Does your proposal meet the client's and stakeholder's needs?
3. Who else is quoting on this project?
4. Critically review your tasks to determine if the outcome of your plan will address every aspect of the project as described.
5. Have you used good grammar and spelling?
6. Is the proposal too long?
7. Is there sufficient amount of information to understand what you are doing and why.
8. Does your proposal use a lot of technical jargon? Define industry key terms if they are necessary to include. Be sure that your impact statement can be understood by anyone.
9. Have you shown that you have everything in place to accomplish project goals?
10. Do you have all the skills or knowledge needed and have you stated this? Clarify your knowledge level. Either show that you have the needed skills or indicate how you will gain these skills or knowledge.
11. Is the proposal overly ambitious, unfeasible or vague?
12. Does the plan include each necessary step to archive the goals and objectives?
13. Have you broken down your project plan into a specific time-line?
14. Have you allowed sufficient contingency?
15. Is your budget overly general or are specific items over-estimated or under-estimated? Get estimates for materials, supplies, and travel.
16. Does your budget make sense for your time-line and tasks and are your expenses appropriate for you project?
17. What will your competitors quote?
18. Are your benefits to the client stated.
19. Are you differentiated from your competitors clearly.
20. Have you stated clearly why you are the best designer to do the job?
21. Is information where a client will expect to see it?
22. Is all information needed to understand the proposal? If not take it out!
23. Can I realistically get everything done in the time-frame I've given?
24. Is the writing clear?
25. Do the ideas make sense?
26. Are all of the requirements fulfilled?
27. Did I avoid repetition?

ONE THING I LEARNED I'VE BEEN IN PRACTICE NOW FOR HALF A CENTURY OR MORE AND THE MOST IMPORTANT INGREDIENT FOR AN ARCHITECT TO DO A GOOD BUILDING IS TO HAVE A GOOD CLIENT. I THINK A CLIENT COUNTS FOR AS MUCH AS FIFTY PER CENT.

I. M. PEI
Chinese-American architect

02
THE DESIGN PROCESS

THE DESIGN PROCESS

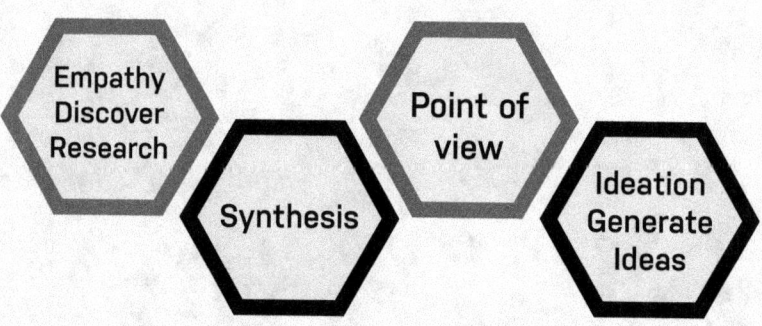

Empathize

Develop a deep understanding of your customers or end users through engaging them and using ethnographic research methods

Synthesize

Make sense from your research. What are the insights? What is connected? What are the unmet needs and desires of your audience?

POV

Define the need you will fulfill with your design. Define the problem that you will solve.

Ideation

Create 75 to 120 potential design solutions. Select the best solutions from the point of view of people, technology and business.

Methods

Innovation
Diagnostic
Warming up
WWWWWH
Interviews
Observation
Focus Groups
Day in the life

Methods

Affinity diagrams
Mind Maps
Persona
Perceptual Maps
Empathy Maps
Experience Maps

Methods

Five Whys
SWOT
Re-framing
Smart Goals
Checklists
Perceptual Maps

Methods

Brainstorming
635 Method
Lotus Method
Scenarios
SCAMPER
Dot Voting

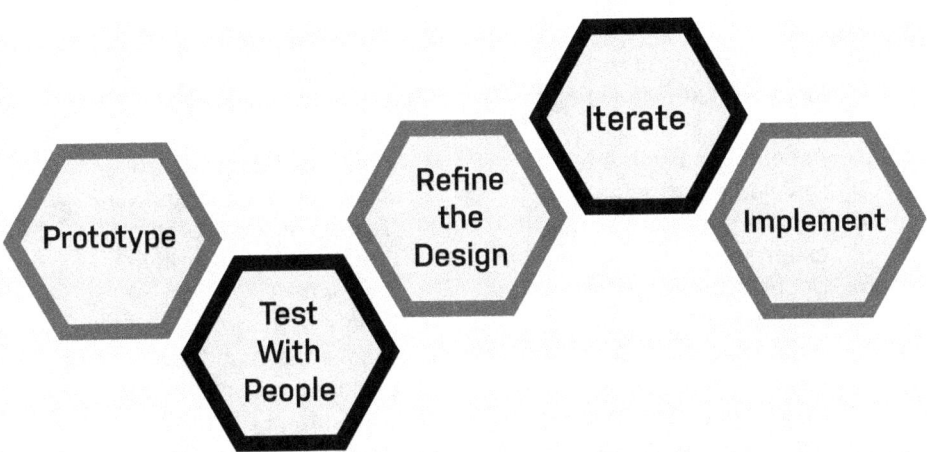

Prototype	Test	Refine	Iterate	Implement
Create a series of fast prototypes to test your design direction	Get feedback from end users and a variety of stakeholders	Refine your design based on the feedback from end users.	Modify the prototype and test and refine as many times as necessary to make your design work.	Manufacture your design. Distribute it and sell it.
Methods	**Methods**	**Methods**	**Methods**	**Methods**
Low Fidelity Dark Horse Video Prototyping Story Board Being your user Wire frames	Method Wizard of Oz Heuristic Evaluation Pictives Creative toolkit	Refine your design based on the feedback from end users.	Modify the prototype and test and refine as many times as necessary to make your design work.	Manufacture your design. Distribute it and sell it.

DESIGN PROCESS

1. GOALS
What are we looking for?
1. Meet with key stakeholders to set vision
2. Assemble a diverse team
3. Develop intent and vision
4. Explore scenarios of user experience
5. Document user performance requirements
6. Define the group of people you are designing for. What is their gender, age, and income range. Where do they live. What is their culture?
7. Define your scope and constraints
8. Identify a need that you are addressing. Identify a problem that you are solving.
9. Identify opportunities
10. Meet stakeholders

2. DISCOVER EMPATHIZE RESEARCH
What else is out there?
1. Identify what you know and what you need to know.
2. Document a research plan
3. Benchmark competitive products
4. Create a budgeting and plan.
5. Create tasks and deliverables
6. Explore the context of use
7. Understand the risks
8. Observe and interview individuals, groups, experts.
9. Develop design strategy
10. Undertake qualitative, quantitative, primary and secondary research.
11. Talk to vendors

3. SYNTHESIZE
What have we learned?
1. Review the research.
2. Make sense out of the research
3. Develop insights
4. Cluster insights
5. Create a hierarchy

4. A UNIQUE POINT OF VIEW
Who are we designing for?
What is their unmet need?
Why do the need it?

5. IDEATE
How is this for as a starting point?
1. Brainstorm
2. Define the most promising ideas
3. Refine the ideas
4. Establish key differentiation of your ideas
5. Investigate existing intellectual property.

6. PROTOTYPE TEST ITERATE
How could we make it better?
1. Make your favored ideas physical.
2. Create low-fidelity prototypes from inexpensive available materials
3. Develop question guides
4. Develop test plan
5. Test prototypes with stakeholders
6. Get feedback from people.
7. Refine the prototypes
8. Test again
9. Build in the feedback
10. Refine again.
11. Continue iteration until design works.
12. Document the process.
13. When you are confident that your idea works make a prototype that looks and works like a production product.

7. IMPLEMENT AND DELIVER
Let's make it. Let's sell it.
1. Create your proposed production design
2. Test and evaluate
3. Review objectives
4. Manufacture your first samples
5. Review first production samples and refine.
6. Launch
7. Obtain user feedback
8. Conduct field studies
9. Define the vision for the next product or service.

PLANNING PHASE

WHAT IS IT?
One of the critical factors for project success is having a good project plan. The plan is a roadmap for the project created through discussions with stakeholders.

HOW TO PLAN A DESIGN PROJECT
1. Study the project assignment carefully.
2. Think about what your final result will look like. Will it be a physical product, or a digital one? Will it involve a service?
3. Select you team.
4. Define a project space.
5. Define team roles and responsibilities.
6. Develop project vision and strategy
7. Determine the activities
8. How team makes decisions
9. Develop team communication plan.
10. Develop a scope statement.
11. Plan the activities in time.
12. Identify important milestones
13. Determine and identify interdepencies between your activities
14. Develop the schedule and cost estimates.
15. Create management plan.
16. Analyze project risks.
17. Develope reporting plan.
18. Plan how project information will be stored and how different stakeholders can access it.

SMART GOALS

SPECIFIC
The desired results should be formulated specifically, and not too generally.

MEASURABLE
The results should be formulated in a way that it is possible to measure whether they have been completed. 'I will produce minimal 5 ideas' instead of 'I will produce several ideas'

ACCEPTABLE
Be sure that there is consensus (among the members of your team or with your tutor) on what the results entail or try to accomplish.

REALISTIC
Results should be feasible; they can be completed in the scope of the project.

TIME
When will the project milstones will be completed?

Source: wikid.eu

End sections of proposal   47

During this phase we investigate our users needs. We need to understand the context that surrounds the product. We use a variety of research techniques to investigate the user needs and the product context.

PROJECT VISION
What is your vision for this product?
What defines success for this project?
What are the potential hurdles?

CUSTOMERS & STAKEHOLDERS
What are the different types of stakeholders?
Who is primary user?
What is the background of the typical user?

VALUE PROPOSITION
What problems do users have that this product solves?
What unmet need is the product meeting?
What is the unique value proposition?

COMPETITION
What similar products are in use today?
What are their relative strengths/weaknesses opportunities & threats?
How is this offering different and unique?

CONTEXT OF USE
What products do they use today?
How do they use these products?
What's missing that this product can provide?
What is the system of products and services that this product will be part of?

USER GOALS
What defines success?
What defines failure?
What do users desire most?

DISCOVERY PHASE

WHAT IS IT?
During this phase we investigate our users unmet needs.
What are they currently doing? What constraints are there?

In order to design a service effectively we need to understand the context that surrounds the service. We use a variety of research techniques to investigate the user needs and the service context.

By the end of this phase we will have an overview of user needs, existing services and their effectiveness and have a foundation to explore possible design directions. We will explore these areas through a variety of research methods

TIMESCALES
The exact length of time required will relate to the design problems being explored.

OUTPUTS
Outputs of this phase could include:
1. A list of user needs
2. A list of user unmet needs
3. A hierarchy of user needs
4. A plan for the resources required to complete the project.
5. the ability to scope and plan an alpha
6. A decision to progress to next phase
7. Perhaps a low fidelity prototype or several low fidelity prototypes.
8. Four to six personas
9. A list of the most important stakeholders both internally in your organization and externally.
10. A benchmarking of existing or competitive services and a SWOT analysis of these services.
11. A definition of the target audience.

Adapted from Discovery phase Government Service Design Manual, https://www.gov.uk/service-manual/phases/discovery (accessed July 06, 2016).

THE DISCOVERY PROCESS

ASSEMBLE YOUR TEAM
Select a diverse cross disciplinary group of people. Have different disciplines, different genders, ages, cultures, represented for the most successful results. Have some T shaped people. These are people who have more than one area of experience or training such as design and management. They will help your team collaborate productively.

DEFINE YOUR TARGET AUDIENCE
Creating a projected user models will keep the development team rooted to a realistic user requirements and minimizes user frustration with the real product. Having a deep understanding of users can help development team better understand the wants & needs of the targeted customers. This will help the development team relate better with the target user. Understanding user tasks helps in developing design solutions that will ensure that the user expectations are met & avoid design errors and customer frustration. Use research methods such as interviewing, observation, empathy maps and user experience maps to better understand your audience. Market segmentation is basically the division of market into smaller segments. It helps identify potential customers and target them.

TYPES OF SEGMENTATION
1. Behavior segmentation
2. Benefit segmentation
3. Psychographic segmentation
4. Geographic segmentation
5. Demographic segmentation

1. What is your target group's goals emotions, experiences, needs and desires?
2. Information collected from just a few people is unlikely to be representative of the whole range of users.
3. What are the user tasks and activities?
4. How will the user use the product or service to perform a task?
5. What is the context of the user?
6. Where are they? What surrounds them physically and virtually or culturally?
7. How large is your user group?

When defining your target audience consider:
1. Age
2. Gender
3. Occupation
4. Industry
5. Travel
6. Citizenship status
7. Marital status
8. Income
9. Culture
10. Occupation
11. Language
12. Religion

13. Location
14. Education
15. Nationality
16. Mobility
17. Migration
18. Mental state
19. Abilities
20. Disabilities
21. Health

IDENTIFY THE STAKEHOLDERS
1. Identify and document a list of stakeholders
2. Determine internal stakeholders
3. Identify and document external stakeholders
4. Prioritize the stakeholders by participation or importance
5. Determine stakeholders specific interests and needs
6. Evaluate stakeholder influence
7. Create a process for communicating with all stakeholders
8. Prepare a stakeholder management plan.
9. Prepare a stakeholder communication plan
10. Define responsibilities
11. Define which stakeholders will be participating at different stages in the project
12. Obtain stakeholder buy-in

IDENTIFY OPPORTUNITIES

SELECT RESEARCH METHODS
Design research is useful to understand your end users perspective and their behaviors. The methods chapter in this book describes many commonly used methods of getting to know your users and their contexts.

DOCUMENT A RESEARCH PLAN
1. What information do you need to inform the design process?
2. Why do you want to answer this question
3. How do you plan on discovering it?
4. Who should you interview?
5. Why do you select these people?
6. How do you gain access to these people?
7. What are your biases about this topic?
8. How do you reduce bias?
9. What methods will you use to inform the design process?
10. How do you know if you can trust what you find?
11. How will you find people you can trust to help you learn?
12. How will you share the information?

SHARE WHAT YOU KNOW

1. In the project kick off meeting ask every team member to introduce themselves and to describe in 3 minutes what experience they have that may be relevant to the project.
2. The moderator can list areas of knowledge on a white board.

IDENTIFY WHAT YOU NEED TO KNOW

Arrange a project kick-off meeting. Invite your team and important stakeholders. On a white board or flip chart create two lists.

Ask each person to introduce themselves and describe what they know or have experienced that may be useful for implementing the project. Brainstorm with your group the areas that are unknown and how that information may be obtained. Formulate a research plan and assign responsibilities, tasks and deliverables with dates.

UNCOVER NEEDS

1. "What causes the problem?"
2. "What are the impacts of the problem?"
3. ""What are possible solutions?"
4. Probe about workarounds How do people adapt their environment to solve problems that they have?
5. Ask what their single biggest obstacle is to achieve what they are trying to achieve How can you help them?
6. Ask what's changing in their world. What are the trends?
7. Observe people
8. Can you see problems they have that they perhaps do not even recognize are problems?
9. Ask other stakeholders

DEFINE THE GOALS

A goal is the intent or intents of the design process.

1. Write a detailed description of the design problem.
2. Define a list of needs that are connected to the design problem.
3. Make a list of obstacles that need to be overcome to solve the design problem.
4. Make a list of constraints that apply to the problem.
5. Rewrite the problem statement to articulate the above requirements.

UNCOVER PEOPLES STORIES

A powerful story can help ensure the success of a new product, service or experience. Storytelling can be an effective method of presenting a point of view. Research can uncover meaningful stories from end that illustrate needs or desires. These stories can become the basis of new designs or actions and be used to support decisions. Stories can be an effective way of communicating complex ideas and inspiring people to change.

1. The stories help to get buy-in from people throughout the design process and may be used to help sell a final design.
2. Real life stories are persuasive.
3. They are different to advertising because they are able to influence a design if uncovered from users during the early research phases and provide authenticity.

CHALLENGES

1. A story with too much jargon will lose an audience.
2. Not everyone has the ability to tell vivid stories.
3. Stories are not always generalizable.

AN EFFECTIVE STORY

1. Meets information needs for your audience
2. Offers a new vantage point
3. Is a real world story
4. Evokes the future
5. Share emotion
6. Communicate transformations
7. Communicate who you are.
8. Describes actions
9. Shows cause and effect
10. Speaks from your experience.
11. Shares your passion
12. Is honest
13. Builds trust
14. Transmits values
15. Shares a vision
16. Shares knowledge
17. Differentiates you.
18. Uses humor
19. Engages the audience
20. Craft the story for your audience.
21. Pose a problem and offer a resolution
22. The audience must be able to act on your story.

SYNTHESIS

SYNTHESIS
Synthesis is a convergent part of the design process. In this stage we review the research, make connections, uncover insights, distill the data. We make sense of the information

ACTIONABLE INSIGHTS
An insight is a fresh point of view based on a deep understanding of the way of thinking and behavior of the end user. An insight occurs by connecting two or more things that have not been connected before. These may be things that many people have seen or experienced but not connected before. The goal is to build actionable insights that can lead to design solutions

USER NEED STATEMENT
The user need statement or question is the desires or needs of end users expressed in their own words.

User Need Statement:
I am a doctor who has a hard time keeping babies warm.

POINT OF VIEW STATEMENT
A point-of-view (POV) is reframing of a design challenge into an actionable problem statement. The POV is used as the basis for design ideation. The POV defines the design intent.

The POV helps reframe he design problem into an actionable focus for the generation of ideas.

"There are several immediate ways to begin to understand the gathered data.
1. Externalize the process.
2. Basic visual design begins to clean up the mess.
3. Organization helps identify relationships
4. Make relationships explicit in plain language
5. Interpret gathered data through alternative visualizations. Enhance the content through "best guess" intuitive leaps"

Information Architecture and Design Strategy: The Importance of Synthesis during the Process of Design Jon Kolko, Savannah College of Art and Design

IDEATION

Once you have identified your target audience unmet needs, the starting point of ideation phase is the problem statement.

[customer] XXXX [Needs] XXXX because XXXX[insight]

Now you can start generating ideas. Find a good space with natural lighting a large table and some white boards.

Your most productive creative team is a diverse group of people. Have different genders, cultures, ages and professions represented. Between four and eight people is the ideal team size for ideation. A larger team becomes harder to manage. Before you start, review the insights and themes from the previous synthesis stage.

Try to generate as many ideas as possible. At first it is good to explore wild blue sky directions. You can always pull the ideas back to reality and budgets as they are refined. We like to generate around 100 to 120 ideas as a starting point. Then narrow them down to around seven preferred directions by combining and developing the ideas through several stages of iteration.

Physical prototypes will allow you to make intangible ideas tangible so that you can get feedback and discuss alternative concept directions.

Service designers use a range of techniques which include sketches, scenarios, video, body storming, paper prototypes, wireframes and PICTIVES to explore and create low fidelity prototypes of ideas.

Make sure that you have ample display space. Sheets of foam core board make low cost pin boards. Put a box of post its and markers in the center of a large table to be shared by the group.

WHEN IDEATING
1. Defer judgment
2. Encourage wild ideas
3. Build on ideas of others (and not but)
4. Stay focused
5. Be visual
6. One conversation
7. Go for quantity

Use different techniques to generate ideas, not just one

PROTOTYPING

WHAT IS PROTOTYPING PHASE?
First make your ideas tangible with a series of fast, inexpensive prototypes. Then progress to higher fidelity prototypes. Building prototypes is making ideas tangible.Prototypes enable the designer to share ideas with others, get feedback Should be made quickly, changed without repercussions Easy to edit, elicit better feedback and learn how to improve the design.
Prototyping filters the details that designers are interested in without distorting the understanding of the whole.

Ask people to give you feedback and use it to improve the designs. Focus on the 20% of the functionality that will be used 80% of the time. Rapid prototyping does not have to be perfect, just enough to give everyone a common understanding.

If you build a high fidelity prototype too early
You will become emotionally attached to your designs
Will be hesitant to change them
Even when they are unusable

WHY PROTOTYPE?
- Designers sometimes start with a bad idea.
- Prototypes help you ensure that the design is right when it is time to ship.
- Prototyping helps designers make usable designs

WHAT TO PROTOTYPE
Complex interactions
new functionality, changes in workflow new technology
new materials.

"The best prototype is the one that in the simplest and most efficient manner makes the possibilities and limitations of a design visible and measurable."
Source:Tochi

HOW TO PROTOTYPE
- One approach is to start prototyping broadly and widely and then dive deep into selected areas of the solution.
- Will not be right the first time
- Work collaboratively with users
- They valuable feedback,
- They gain a sense of ownership of the final product.
- Remind everyone, including yourself, that rapid

- prototyping is a means to an end, not an end in itself.
- Don't prototype features or functionality that cannot be implemented.
- Don't take every change or request that comes out of a prototype review as a new requirement.
- Don't begin prototype review sessions without clear guidelines for feedback. Be very specific about the type of feedback you are looking for.
- Build the level of fidelity that allows you to test what's important while
- maximizing the number of possible iterations.
- You may also need to construct part of the "context of use"
- in addition to the product being designed
- Consider the context of use of the final product or service.
- Prototype the variables that need the most attention or are vital to
- the user achieving their goal.
- Introduce your prototype as a work in progress.
- Integrate feedback.
- For service prototypes people and their activities and experiences are more important than the phycical objects
- Horizontal prototyping. Broad shows design in a shallow manner.
- Vertical prototyping. Some features simulated in detail.

Source: Kolko

TESTING

- Test your prototypes with 2 or 3 users in the context of use
- Ask the user to imagine that they are in the appropriate context
- Tell they user they are going to be completing a familiar task with your prototype
- Describe the task to them. Provide the prototype.
- Ask them to walk you through the act of using it
- Record everything.
- Use video or audio, and camera
- Have one person dedicated to taking notes and
- Have one person dedicated to taking photos or video.
- Ask the user to talk as much as possible while performing the task
- Verbalize their thoughts
- Refine your prototypes so that they "solve" the problem.
- Refine your prototype to address the primary failpoints and test it again.
- Repeat this process

TYPES OF MODELS

3D SKETCH MODEL
3D sketch models are 3D visual design representations that represent an idea.

DESIGN DEVELOPMENT MODEL
Design development models are 3D visual design representations used to understand the relationships between

APPEARANCE MODEL
Appearance models are 3d visual design representations used to understand the relationships between components, cavities, interfaces, structure and form.

FUNCTIONAL CONCEPT MODEL
Functional concept models are 3D visual design representations that show functionality and highlight important functional parameters including yield and performance factors.

CONCEPT OF OPERATION MODEL
Concept of operation models are 3D visual design representations that help communicate an understanding of the operational strategies and usage procedures relating to the product.

PRODUCTION CONCEPT MODEL
Production concept models are 3D visual design representations used to help assist the evaluation of production processes or manufacturing technologies for final

ASSEMBLY CONCEPT MODEL
Assembly concept models are 30 visual design representations that provide confidence regarding the component relationships in terms of assembly, cost and investment.

SERVICE CONCEPT MODEL
Service concept models are 30 visual design representations that illustrate how the product may be serviced or maintained.

TYPES OF PROTOTYPES

APPEARANCE PROTOTYPE
Appearance prototypes are highly detailed, full-scale visual design representations that combine function and aesthetics.

ALPHA PROTOTYPE
Alpha prototypes are 3D visual design representations used to verify the outlook and construction of sub-systems that have been individually proven and accepted with the materials aesthetics and layout for the product

BETA PROTOTYPE
beta prototypes are full-scale and fully-functional 3D visual design representations constructed from the actual materials and used to examine how the product would be used in its intended environment and to work out regulatory issues.

PRE-PRODUCTION PROTOTYPE
pre-production prototypes are final 3D visual design representations used to check the product and its finishing as a whole and to perform production and assembly assessment in small batches.

EXPERIMENTAL PROTOTYPE
Experimental prototypes are 3D visual design representations that parameterizes the layout or shape of a product, usually to replicate the actual product's physics.

SYSTEM PROTOTYPE
System prototypes are 3D visual design representations that combines the numerous components specified for the final product to test and assess functional aspects such as mechanism and performance

FINAL HARDWARE PROTOTYPE
Final hardware prototypes are 3D visual design representations used to assist in the design and evaluation of product fabrication and other assembly issues.

SCENARIOS

PAPER PROTOTYPES

STORYBOARD
The storyboard is a tool from cinema. It is used to represent a customer experience through a series of drawings or pictures, put together in a narrative sequence.

FOAM MODEL
Urethane foam product models are a cost-effective way to evaluate multiple design concepts prior to the finalization of a design. CNC Foam prototypes can be easily sanded and modified to fine-tune a design.

DESK TOP WALKTHROUGH
Desktop walkthrough simple exercises in imagining a user experience using small, hand sized figures. A typical desktop walkthrough involves a customer, a member of staff, an environment and some paper touch points." These desktop artefacts can be considered representations of experiencescapes.

VIDEO PROTOTYPE
A video explaining your service of user experience idea.

ROLEPLAY
Act out your idea in front of an audience or camera.

STORYBOARD
Describe how the user interacts with your idea

SCALE MODEL
Show form, arrangement and working at a smaller scale.

VIRTUAL/AUGMENTED REALITY
Use projections or VR goggles for an immersive experience.

PRODUCT HACK
Make adjustments to an existing product.

FEASIBILITY PROTOTYPE
Determine feasibility of various solutions Proof of concept for specific

OPERATIONAL MODEL
Performs desired functionalities for usability testing.

APPEARANCE MODEL
Accurate physical representation of product appearance.

USABILITY TEST TIME-LINE

Test–2 weeks	Determine test audience, start recruiting
Test–2 weeks	Determine feature set to be tested
Test–1 week	Write first version of guide, discuss with team, check on recruiting
Test–3 days	Write second version of guide, recruiting should be completed
Test–2 days	Complete guide, schedule practice test, set up and check equipment
Test–1 day	Do practice test in the morning, adjust guide/tasks as appropriate
Test	Test (usually 1-2 days, depending on scheduling)
Test+1 day	Discuss with observers, collect copies of all notes
Test+3 days	Watch all tapes, take notes
Test+1 week	Combine notes, write analysis
Test+1 week	Present to team, discuss and note directions for further research

Source: Adaptive Path

USABILITY TESTING

WHAT IS USABILITY TESTING?
Usability testing helps improve a design to make it more usable. Real users undertake particular tasks. Researchers and other stakeholders observe and collect data.

GOALS
Meet with stakeholders, to define your goals.
1. Who uses the product or service?
2. What are their needs and goals?
3. What tasks does the user need to perform?
4. Where are the problems?

PROCESS
1. Develop a test plan
2. Choose a testing space
3. Recruit participants
4. Prepare test materials
5. Conduct the tests
6. Debrief participants
7. Analyze data
8. Conclusions and recommendations

WHAT TO TEST
1. Low-fidelity prototype or paper prototype
2. Wireframes
3. High-fidelity prototype and experience system.
4. Alpha and Beta prototypes·

5. Test competitor's designs
6. Test in the real context of use.
7. Test iteratively
8. Use heuristics and usability guidelines.
9. Test the final design

HOW MANY TO TEST
Test at least four people from each user group.

DIAGNOSTIC EVALUATION
1. Test 4-6 users
2. Find and fix problems
3. During design development
4. Test iteratively

SUMMATIVE TESTING
1. How many? 6-12 users
2. Metrics based on usability goals
3. Test to measure the success of a design.
4. When At end of process
5. Test once

Source: Ginny Redish

DESIGN THE TEST
Document your test plan checklist Test participants tasks under controlled conditions.

WHERE
Usability tests can take place in a lab, conference room, quiet office

space, or a quiet public space.

SCENARIOS AND TASKS
Tasks are the activities that your participants undertake. Scenarios frame tasks and provide motivation.

TIPS FOR WRITING SCENARIOS
Start with a scenario. Scenarios should be a story that provides motivation to your participants. The scenario is a narrative that explains the background of the task in a real world situation. Create believable scenarios. Keep them simple.

WRITING TASKS
Categories:
1. Prescribed tasks. You determine what the participant will do.
2. Participant defined Have them do the task they describe.
3. Open ended Participants organically explore the activity based on a scenario you provide.

SELECT DATA TO CAPTURE
Log:
1. Task start and end points
2. Milestones
3. Errors
4. Failures
5. Problems
6. Requests for help

QUALITATIVE DATA
Record behavior, reactions, language.

SUCCESS PATHS
Is there only one or several success paths?

RECRUIT PARTICIPANTS
Select participants who represent typical novice average and experienced users.

RECRUITMENT IDEAS
1. Contact databases
2. Recruitment agencies
3. Craig's List
4. Your web site
5. Media ads
6. Identify the target criteria for your participants.

SCREENER.
Filter the participants with a screener.

COMPENSATION
Motivate participants with cash, a gift certificate or products.

SETTING
Pick a large room with good natural lighting and low background noise.

SCHEDULE PARTICIPANTS
Allow time for contingencies between sessions.

STAKEHOLDERS
Brief stakeholders that their task is to observe. The facilitator may interact with participants or not interact.

OBSERVERS
Enlist one person to log observations. Create a list of stakeholders. Observing testing helps make the team make improvements to the design. Do not change the design until you understand the meaning of your observations.

SCRIPT
Create a facilitator script.

QUESTIONNAIRES AND SURVEYS
A typically usability study usually has at least two surveys (questionnaires), one administered before the

HOW MANY USERS SHOULD YOU TEST?
Nielsen found that testing 5 users uncovered 85% of problems

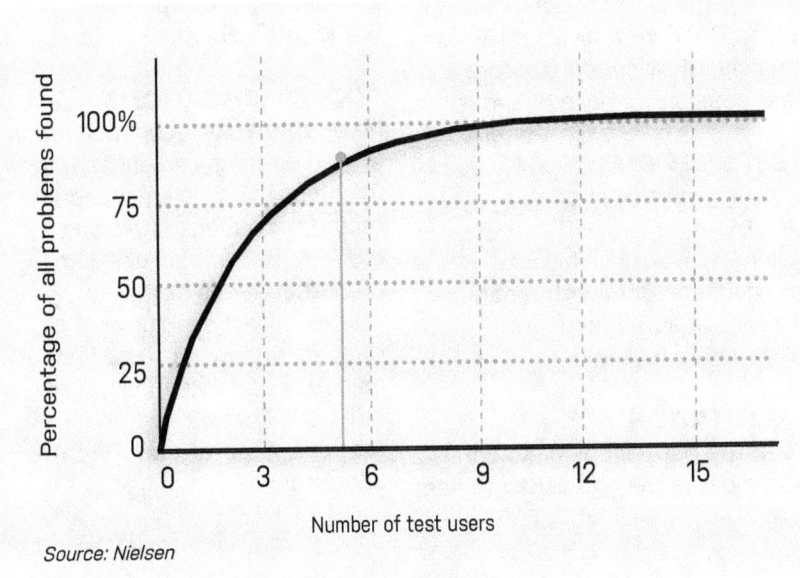

Source: Nielsen

participant starts tasks and one administered at the end of the test,

PRE-TEST SURVEY
collects demographic and product usage data about participants

POST-TASK SURVEY
Questions about the usability and satisfaction related to test tasks. Collect only data that you can legally collect. Use age ranges rather than specific ages when asking participants for their age. Include comment fields

RUN-THROUGH
Run through your test yourself to make sure the tasks make sense Conduct a pilot test with a participant. Allow time before the test session to make changes.

TEST SESSION
Welcome participant
Use the script
Ask participants to fill out the consent form with a non-disclosure agreement.
Allow enough time

FACILITATION
Keep the participant focused.
Participants may be asked to keep a running commentary or "think-aloud" protocol
Ask open ended questions
What are you thinking?
What are you trying to do?
What did you expect to happen?
Keep neutral and do not show emotion, approval or disapproval.

TASK FAILURES
If a participant fails a task ask them to do the task again.

AFTER THE SESSION
Debrief with observers.
Clean the space.

ANALYSIS
1. Review observations
2. Identify problems
3. Identify solutions.

RECOMMENDATIONS
Make sure your recommendations should address the underlying cause of the problem. Keep recommendations short and concise. Use video, wireframes and other visual means to illustrate your conclusions. Recommendations should be objective and evidence based. The usability test of the X Product requires 12 participants from 2 user groups.

Source: Usability Testing Basics. An Overview

DATA ANALYSIS

WHAT IS IT?
Data analysis is the process of making meaning from the data.

CODING
1. Read through the text data. Divide the text into segments of information.
2. Label the segments with codes

CLUSTERING
1. After open coding an entire text, make a list of all code words.
2. Assign a code word or phrase that accurately describes the meaning of the text segment (30 to 40 codes)
3. Objective: reduce the long list of codes to a smaller, more manageable number (25 or 30)
4. Reduce the overlap and redundancy of codes(reduce to 20 codes) Cluster together similar codes and look for redundant codes

THEMES
Themes are similar codes aggregated together to form a major idea. Themes can also be referred to as categories.
The process of looking for categories that cut across all data sets. You can't classify something as a theme unless it cuts across the preponderance of the data.(5 to 7 themes)
This core is a theoretical framework that further guides the research and design process.
Name the themes. The names can come from at least three sources:
The researcher
The participants
Most common: when the researcher comes up with terms, concepts, and categories that reflect what he or she sees in the data
Themes should Reflect the purpose of the research
Be exhaustive--you must place all data in a category

TYPES OF THEMES
1. Ordinary: themes a researcher expects
2. Unexpected: themes that are surprises and not expected to surface
3. Hard-to-classify: themes that contain ideas that do not easily fit into one theme or that overlap with several themes
4. Major & minor themes: Themes that represent the major ideas, or minor, secondary ideas in a database.
5. Codes such as "seating arrangements," "teaching approach," or "physical layout of the room," might all be

used to describe a classroom where instruction takes place

DISPLAY THE DATA VISUALLY
1. Comparison table or matrix
2. Hierarchical tree diagram that represents themes and their connections
3. Boxes that show connections between themes
4. Physical layout of the setting
5. Personal or demographic information for each person or site

VALIDATE YOUR FINDINGS
1. Prolonged engagement & persistent observation in the field
2. Triangulation
3. Peer Review
4. Clarifying researcher bias
5. Member Checking
6. Rich, thick description
7. External Audit

"In qualitative research, a single case or small nonrandom sample is selected precisely because the researcher wishes to understand the particular in depth, not to find out what is generally true of the many" (Merriam, 1998, p. 208).

TRIANGULATION
Use of two or more independent sources of data or data collection methods to corroborate research findings within a study. The researcher looks for patterns of convergence to develop or corroborate an overall interpretation

REPORT
Write a qualitative report providing detailed information about a few themes rather than general information about many themes. Written account should include sufficient data to allow the reader to judge whether the interpretation offered is adequately supported by the data

ITERATION

WHAT IS ITERATION?
Iteration is the process of reworking and refining your design. The level of reworking and refining determines the final quality and the usability of your design for customers of end users. Show your prototype to end users and based on their feedback make iterative improvements.

Steps of iterative design process are as follows:
1. Complete an initial design
2. Create a low fidelity prototype.
3. Present the design to a minimum of 5 test users
4. Identify any problems experienced by the test user
5. Refine the design to fix the problems
6. Repeat steps 2-5 until all design problems are resolved

BENEFITS OF TESTING
1. Identify how long it takes to complete tasks
2. Find out if participants like your design
3. Identify changes required to improve user performance and satisfaction
4. And analyse the performance to see if it meets your objectives

IDENTIFY STAKEHOLDERS
A stakeholder is anyone or any organization that will be affected by your design including end users, suppliers and people within your client's organization.

OBTAIN FEEDBACK
Usability testing is undertaken to evaluate a product or service by testing it on users. Usability testing focuses on measuring a designs fitness for an intended purpose. Usability testing involves observation under controlled conditions to determine how well people can use the design

Feedback methods include:
1. Remote usability testing
2. Expert reviews
3. Individual In-depth Interviews
4. Focus groups
5. Card Sorting
6. Paper prototyping
7. Usability lab testing
8. Eyetracking
9. A/B Testing. Two versions (A and B) are compared, which are identical except for one variation that might impact a user's behaviour.
10. Click tracking

TEST AND EVALUATE
The design team checks design capabilities, requirements by testing with end users and the ability to meet these, and epitomizing the design to combine these two.

FINALIZE YOUR DESIGN
The details of this phase will depend on the type of design area that you are working in.

BUILD EXTERNAL PARTNERSHIPS
Collaboration with other organizations and individuals is an integral part of the design process. Organizations benefit from their partners' insights and expertise. Many of the best ideas have emerged not through the inspiration of a single mind, but through the exchange of ideas.

SIGN OFF FROM STAKEHOLDERS
When you believe that you have a design that can be distributed and sold, show it to all your stakeholders one last time before documenting the design for final manufacture.

AUTHORIZE VENDORS
Review beta prototype with vendors

PRE-LAUNCH
1. Create the campaign.
2. Evoke emotion.
3. Create desire.
4. Prepare marketing materials.
5. Do something original.
6. Review what's working.
7. Create urgency.

LAUNCH
At this point in the design process the design is launched, and the process now includes liaison with appropriate internal teams in areas such as marketing, communications, and brand.
1. How can you reduce the risk of failure?
2. Have you met your goals.
3. Is it compelling?
4. Set a date.

GOING LIVE
You have met the user needs identified in the discovery, alpha and beta testing. Now you are ready to go live.

POST-LAUNCH
1. Have a party!
2. Ask for feedback from first buyers
3. Deliver a bonus that wasn't expected
4. Make it memorable.
5. Review and improve.
6. Plan ahead.

DELIVER

Do final testing obtain sign off from stakeholders and launch. The design should successfully address the problem identified in the user research phase of the process.

Key activities and objectives during the Deliver Stage are:

1. Final testing, approval and launch
2. Targets, evaluation and feedback loops.

DID THE DESIGN MEET IT'S GOALS?

Ideas that have emerged during the design process or in post-launch feedback may be put to one side but developed later, and will then go through the design process again on its own.

MEASURE SUCCESS

1. Determine how you will measure the success
2. 2 to 3 months after release measure the success
3. Measure the success and objectively evaluate.
4. Implement metrics and measurements

SOME WAYS TO MEASURE SUCCESS:

1. Customer satisfaction
2. ROI is standard business measure of project profitability, over the market life of the design expressed as a percentage of initial investment.
3. Increased usage
4. Increased revenue from existing customers
5. The ability of your product to solve the problem
6. New customer acquisition
7. Product margin
8. Cash flow
9. Design team's satisfaction
10. Improved customer retention rate
11. Increased market share

WHAT COULD BE IMPROVED?

Invite customers to co-create, and integrate feedback.

DEFINE NEXT VISION

The design process is never complete. Now it is time to start planning the next design so that you can stay ahead of the many competitors.

Source: Adapted from Jonathan Mead "The 40 Step Checklist for a Highly Successful Launch"

I SUSPECT THAT WRITER'S BLOCK AFFLICTS MAINLY PEOPLE WHO HAVE SOME STABLE AND AMPLE SOURCE OF INCOME OUTSIDE OF WRITING. SO FAR IT HASN'T BEEN A PROBLEM.

FRED SABERHAGEN
American writer

03
ANATOMY OF A PROPOSAL
FORWARD PROPOSAL
SECTIONS

FORWARD PROPOSAL SECTIONS

In this chapter I will discuss the individual parts of a design proposal that are found at the front of a proposal document.

These sections define why the project has been initiated and the design firm's approach to solving the design need. They answer the questions what, why, and how in relation to the project.

You do not provide design solutions here or elsewhere in the proposal but you communicate why you are the best designer to undertake thie project.

In this chapter I discuss the following parts of design proposal.

1. The cover letter
2. The proposal cover page
3. Background or introduction
4. Audience
5. Executive summary
6. Current stuation
7. Goals and objectives
8. Probem or needs statement
9. Competitive analysis
10. Design strategy
11. Value proposition
12. Schedule of meetings

THE COVER LETTER

Sometimes the cover letter is read by a client but it does not interest them enough and the proposal is discarded.

The goal of the cover letter is to hook the client's interest to make them read your proposal.

If you just had two minutes to explain your value to a client what would you say? Use your words carefully and sparingly in the cover letter. Conclude the cover letter with a compelling call to action. Make it positive and engaging. Substantiate your claims. List next steps to get the project underway.

HOW LONG SHOULD IT BE?

The cover letter is best kept brief. The best length is about half a page. It should not be longer than one page.

PROCESS OF WRITING A COVER LETTER

- Your cover letter should be written on business stationery with your corporate identity.
- It should have your company name, your name and contact information.
- Address the letter to a person.
- Include the date.
- You can use the recipient's first name if you know them.
- Take a more formal tone if you do not know them by using titles such as Mr or Ms.
- Close the letter with: Regards if you do not know th recipient , or Sincerely, if you know the reader.
- Define the need that they have that you are addressing.
- Support you claims in your cover letter.
- Start with a statement like "We are excited to have the chance to submit a proposal that will help your company become more competitive in ...."
- If you are sending a cold proposal,you

need a strong and intriguing initial statement.
- Refer if possible to similar projects and quantify their success.
- If they have asked for the proposal start with a statement such as: As per our discussion on June 26, we are presenting our design proposal to.....
- Quantify or otherwise define with evidence the value that you bring
- Bullet point four or five points to define your goals.
- State the benefits that you will provide for the reader and for their organization.
- "Our design will improve your profitability in sporting products by 35%."
- State your qualifications in a short paragraph including your years of experience, projects, products and clients.

CALL TO ACTION!
- At the end of the letter clearly define the next steps to jet the project underway.
- To initiate the project return to us an original copy of the signed authorization to proceed, with your official company order for stage one for $28,000 and a deposit of $14,000."
- Ask them to contact you with questions
- "After reviewing the proposal, please do contact me at 616-205-7089 to answer any questions that you may have."
- "I will follow up with you on Monday to discuss any questions that you may have and the possibility of working together.
- Ask two people in your office to proodf read the proposal and cover letter before sending it.

EXAMPLE OF A COVER LETTER

DESIGN COMMUNITY COLLEGE INC.
PO Box 1153
Topanga CA 90290 USA

Dear Peter

This is our project proposal with our estimate based on our discussions and past projects.

We can commence work on our current schedule within seven days of receiving the following:
1. The official authorization to proceed which you will find on page 14 of the attached proposal signed by one of your company directors.
2. Your company order foir the value of stage one $28,000.
3. The deposit for stage one $14,000.

The remaining balance we will invoice based on work undertaken each month. Expenses including materials and travel will be invoiced at a rate of cost plus twenty-five percent as they are incurred. Travel will be blled at fifty percent of our usual hourly for a maximum of eight hours per day. Materials will not exceed ten percent of total billing.

We look forward to working with you to make this project a success. If you need more information please contact me at 616-304-8675.

Sincerely,

PROPOSAL COVER PAGE

The cover page of a business proposal creates a first impression that can encourage or discourage an evaluator from continuing. Create a template for this page that you can use on your proposals. The cover page should look clean and organized. Consider it to be part of your portfolio. The fonts should be larger than ten points to be readable. Fonts and layout should be consistent with your other documents such as your cover letter, portfolio and business card.

Give every possible method to reach you on the cover. Postal address, office 'phone, email and Web address. Mobile 'phone numbers are optional, but include them if they are the easiest way to reach you.

On inside pages Include your email contact and the proposal and issue number on each page in the footer. Number each page and give the total number of pages in the footer of each page.

Include the following information:
1. Your organization's name
2. Logo
3. Design Proposal
4. The title of the project
5. Date of the submission
6. Your contact details
7. Your client contact details
8. Length of project validity
9. Proposal number
10. Issue Number
11. Confidentiality notice

CONFIDENTIALITY NOTICE
Make it clear that your proposal should not be shown to others especially other designers by including a confidentiality notice on the cover.

"This proposal should be considered private and confidential and may not be shared with any third party without the prior written permission of your company"

AXIS DESIGN

Creativity with strategy

Design Proposal for:
Digital Communication Device
Date: June 16th 2018
Proposal valid to August 16th 2018
Proposal Number: JK 3204
Version: 1-061618

Prepared by:
Todd Janiskson
Axis Design LLC
2021 Old Topanga Blvd
Topanga CA 90290 USA
Office Phone: 616-463-6783
Cell Phone: 616-538-1847
Email tjanisksonn@axisdesign.net

Prepared for:
Jason McDermott
Agile Technologies LLC
22 Technology Drive
Palo Alto CA 94301 USA
Phone: 319-926-4756
Email: jmcdemott@agetec.com

This proposal should be considered private and confidential and may not be shared with any third party without the prior written permission of Axis Design LLC.

DEFINE YOUR AUDIENCE

User-centered design involves making your design compatible with your end user or audience.

1. Useful: Your content should be original and fulfill a need
2. Usable: Design must be easy to use
3. Desirable: Design elements are used to evoke emotion and appreciation
4. Findable: Information should be easy to find
5. Accessible: Content needs to be accessible to people with disabilities
6. Credible: Users must trust and believe what you tell them

Source: www.usability.gov

Before you start your customer research it's critical to know whom you're designing for. Understanding your target audience's needs, contexts, and experiences is essential to design successfully. Consider also the stakeholders. Stakeholders are people or organizations or groups who will be in some way affected by your design.

Define the segment that are your intended customers. Define the customers into groups by factors such as where they live, gender, age, household size, income range, typical level or type of education, occupations, lifestyle, values, culture, language, where they purchase products, benefits sought and level of experience in using this type of product. What's important to them and what motivates them? See the user profile questions in this book. Designers often divide a companies customers into four to six segments. A designer may also create a n archetypal customer for each segment which are called personas.

This section should be between one paragraph to one page. If you are designing for several user segments, define each group in a separate paragraph. Every customer in each group should have one factor in common. Groups can be defined by more than one factor.

DEFINING THE USER PROFILE

Creating a projected user models will keep the development team rooted to a realistic user requirements and minimizes user frustration with the real product. Having a deep understanding of users can help development team better understand the wants & needs of the targeted customers. This will help the development team relate better with the target user. Understanding user tasks helps in developing design solutions that will ensure that the user expectations are met & avoid design errors and customer frustration.

Use research methods such as interviewing, observation, empathy maps and user experience maps to better understand your audience.

Market segmentation is basically the division of market into smaller segments. It helps identify potential customers and target them.

The segmentation is carried out by using one of the five strategies:
1. Behavior segmentation
2. Benefit segmentation
3. Psychographic segmentation
4. Geographic segmentation
5. Demographic segmentation

EXECUTIVE SUMMARY

Show empathy for what is important to the client. Show the client that their objectives are clear to you. Clearly and concisely summarize the key points of the proposal. This may be the only part of your proposal the CEO reads before deciding whether to sign off on your proposal. Make sure your summary is brief, clear and interesting.

WHAT IS AN EXECUTIVE SUMMARY?
The executive summary is your elevator pitch. Convince your reader that they need to invest in you. It is usually located at the beginning of a proposal but it is the section that you should write last. Emphasize the main points of your proposal.

The Executive Summary is an overview of the proposal and appears at the beginning of the proposal. Clients will usually go here or to the budget first. Summarize the main reasons for performing the design and the scope of the design that you propose. The purpose of the Executive Summary is to give the reader an overview of what the design need is and what design approach is being proposed to solve the design problem. This section is the most widely read section of the document. A CEO may only read this section and the price summary to decide whether to sign off. It should be well written and carefully proofread.

IN THIS SECTION
1. Identify the client and the design company.
2. Include at least one sentence with evidence why the design company is the best fit for the project.
3. Include at least one sentence defining the needs being addressed.
4. Include at least one sentence on the goal or objective.
5. Include one sentence defining the strategy.
6. Include at least one sentence on design methods being used
7. Include total cost, and amount requested in the proposal.

EXAMPLE OF AN EXECUTIVE SUMMARY

Smith LLC will design the Osteonexus 2020, a microgravity fracture healing system for NASA. Smith LLC have 30 years experience developing three similar devices for the international space station. The need for this device is as follows: Microgravity environment severely inhibits normal bone healing mechanisms

NASA has identified several design objectives as listed below in order of importance:
1. Effective fracture fixation and healing
2. Ease of use with minimal medical training
3. Maximization of mobility during treatment
4. Small size and low weight

The applied micro-movement will mimic partial load bearing, which has been proven to help heal bone fractures on Earth. The design solution will be developed through prototyping and user testing in a low gravity simulator at NASA. The total cost for stages 1 and 2 will be $142,000.

Source: Adapted from Rice University

> Clients will usually go here or to the budget first The executive who signs off on your proposal may only read this section and the schedule of fees.
>
> Explain your understanding of the client, their business and the industry they operate in. Show the client that their objectives are clear to you.

HOW LONG SHOULD THIS SECTION BE?

It should be short. Don't waste words. The length depends on the complexity of your proposal. Between one paragraph and half a page or less is preferred. The Executive Summary shouldn't be more than about three or four paragraphs. Try to make every point such as the seven key elements of a pitch in three sentences or fewer. It could be up to one or two pages for a complex project.

CURRENT SITUATION

IN THIS SECTION
You may approach the current situation by focusing your writing in one of three ways:

HOW LONG SHOULD THIS SECTION BE?
This section should be between one paragraph to one page.

CAUSAL APPROACH
use this approach if you feel your audience does not already know the
causes of a problem or opportunity.

EFFECTS APPROACH
use this approach to describe what will happen if action is not taken to confront the problem or realize the opportunity.

NARRATIVE APPROACH
whereas the other two approaches are best for describing the situation
as it stands in the present moment, the narrative approach works to show how an opportunity or problem evolved over time
Source: Generic proposal structure ndsu.edu

EXAMPLE OF A CURRENT SITUATION STATEMENT

Anaesthesiologists use a device to stabilize an ultrasound image during regional blocking procedures. In addition to enabling a steady image, the device provides the opportunity to perform ultrasound guided blocks to private practice clinicians for whom the cost of hiring additional staff to use ultrasound technology is prohibitive.

The first iteration of this device which has recently gone to market is manually controlled and relies on friction in ball and socket joints to maintain a "locked" configuration when the target image is acquired. With this implementation, it is easy to ensure that the device holds a fixed position in space and can capture meaningful imagery. It may be more desirable for some medical procedures to fix the ultrasound transducer to acquire an image of a moving target, such as a catheter tip, or a hard lesion, as it is manipulated through less dense tissue. This would require a truly "hands-free" solution, wherein the device and its corresponding transducer can track a target image over the course of a procedure.

Several robotic arms exist for medical purposes, however, none have been specifically designed to assist regional blocking procedures.

Source: Thayer School of Engineering at Dartmouth

PROJECT GOALS & OBJECTIVES

GOALS
Meaning: The purpose toward which an endeavour is directed
Time frame: Long term
Measure: Cannot be measured
Example: I want to achieve success in the field of Product Design and do what no one has ever done before.
Type: Intangible:
Action: Specific action
Plan: Broad plan

IN THIS SECTION
The client should be focused on what they want to achieve and this is where you summarize their objectives. Find Out Your Client's Needs. The words Goal and Objective are sometimes confused. What differentiates them is the time frame, and their effect. Both terms suggest a target that it is desired to accomplish.

Goals define an achievement of efforts. Goals are the vision of the project. Objectives are specific targets within the general goal.

Objectives are time related to achieve a certain task. Objectives are measurable activities to achieve goals; the end points envisioned for the proposed project. Tasks in a design project are steps taken to achieve the stated objectives for the project.

Here are some goal questions you can ask:
- What are your long term goals?
- What are your barriers to achieving these goals?
- What business metrics do you use?
- What motivates your customers to choose your company over the competition?
- Who is your ideal customer? Describe them.

HOW LONG SHOULD THIS SECTION BE?
This section should be between one paragraph to one page. List at least three design objectives.

EXAMPLE OF A PROJECT GOALS & OBJECTIVES STATEMENT

PROJECT GOALS

GOAL 1
The ladder should expand the client's overall market by 25% buy 2025.

GOAL 2
The ladder should expand the customer base in Canada over the next five years.

PROJECT OBJECTIVES

OBJECTIVE 1
The ladder should be safe
- The ladder should be stable
- On smooth surfaces and level ground

OBJECTIVE 2
The ladder should be marketable
- To men between 23 and 55 years old
- To women between 23 and 55 years old

OBJECTIVE 3
The ladder should be inexpensive
- Between $60 and $70

OBJECTIVE 4
The ladder should be portable

OBJECTIVES
Meaning: Something that one's efforts or actions are intended to attain or accomplish; purpose; target
Time frame: Short term
Measure: Can be measured
Example: I want to design a phone for you by December
Type: Tangible
Action: Specific action
Plan: Narrow plan

PROBLEM STATEMENT & NEEDS ASSESSMENT

The problem statement needs assessment section should not make unsupported assumptions, should be interesting to read, make a compelling case, be as concise as possible and free of jargon

IN THIS SECTION
Describe the end users, problem or need that the design will address and how you will measure the success of the outcome. How can you meet your client's and their customer's needs better than anyone else?

Address both the end user or customer's needs and the client's needs in this section. Who will be the end users of the design? Give demographic details - age, industry sector, etc. - as well as details of what needs to be considered with regards to these people. What is the context of use of your product? Describe ways that you will know (or measure) when you have solved the problem. Brainstorm all the project's possible goals, needs, and measurable criteria. With your team create a hierarchy of needs to be addressed and build your problem statement. There may be multiple problem statements. Vote to determine which problem to pursue, and how to scope the statement.

Ask the questions Who? What? Where? When? and Why? How?

An effective proposal describes a client's needs and their drivers. To persuade someone, they must believe you understand their needs. Describe the underlying reason for the project. A "fresh new look" isn't a need statement.

HOW LONG SHOULD THIS SECTION BE?
This section should be one paragraph.

EXAMPLE OF A PROBLEM STATEMENT

Do some research and use it to create a problem statement. We have observed that [user/organization] isn't meeting [these goals/needs], due to [this adverse effect]. How might we improve so that our product/service/team/organization is more successful based on [these measurable criteria]?

We have observed that women in the age range 24 to 36 years old living in Chicago are not able to find safe and inexpensive transportation due to poor safety on the train system. How might we increase the number of women traveling on the train by 25% by 2020 by improving the safety of the system?

An important part of your proposal is showing the potential client that you understand their needs and then providing evidence that you're the best choice for the job. This section of the proposal provides the opportunity to show that you have a clear understanding of the issues and will demonstrate your ability to address them.

COMPETITOR ANALYSIS

There is no point in designing something if the design is not as good as something that already exists. Identify the top competitors. Determine what differentiates their products from other offerings. Do a SWOT analysis to understand their strengths, weaknesses, opportunities and threats. Look for gaps where you can provide a solution that fulfills an unmet need.

An investigation and analysis of your competition allows you to assess your competitor's strengths and weaknesses in your marketplace and helps you to choose and implement effective strategies that will maximize your competitive advantage.

PROCESS
1. Identify competitors
2. Market landscape analysis
3. Identify differentiation
4. Identify competitor's strengths and weaknesses, opportunities and threats
5. Rank competitors
6. Benchmark competitors

HOW LONG SHOULD THIS SECTION BE?
This section should be between one paragraph to one page. Who are my top three competitors?

QUESTIONS TO CONSIDER
- Who are your client's competitors?
- Research competitors and review any material that's been supplied to you by your client.
- Where are the holes? What's good? What's bad?
- Where can you position your client for maximum impact?
- Make some phone calls to vendors and suppliers.
- Ask vendors and suppliers perceptions about your client and some of their competitors.

- Has the client done an intellectual property search?
- Document what competitors are doing poorly as well as where they excel.
- Does your target price compare well with your competition's pricing? On what basis am I able to compete?
- What is the range of products and services they offer?
- Are their products or services aimed at satisfying similar target markets?
- Are my competitors profitable?
- Are they expanding? Scaling down?
- How long have they been in business?
- What are their positive attributes in the eyes of customers?
- What are their negative attributes in the eyes of customers?
- How do current customers view us compared to the competition?
- How can I distinguish my company from my competitors?
- Do they have a competitive advantage; if so, what is it?
- What is their marketing strategy?
- What is their promotional strategy?
- What are their pricing structures?
- Do they operate in the same geographic area?
- Have there been any changes in their targeted market segments?
- What is their size? Revenues?

Rate the following as: fair, good or excellent. Our company & competition

1. Price
2. Quality
3. Durability
4. Image/style
5. Value
6. Name Recognition
7. Customer Service
8. Customer Relations
9. Location
10. Convenience
11. Other

Source: Edward Lowe

DESIGN STRATEGY

Demonstrate how your plan will meet objectives to solve a problem or take advantage of an opportunity

WHAT IS DESIGN STRATEGY?
The creative strategy is how you plan the design activities will meet the objectives of the business and the unmet needs and wants of the end users. Show an accurate and complete understanding of the client's needs. Present a practical plan that responds to the the problems that keep the client awake at night. Focus on an approach that emphasizes the client benefits that your proposal has to offer. Provide evidence that you can carry out the plan successfully.

IN THIS SECTION
- Identify needs
- Determine goals
- Figure out a roadmap
- Forecast your major steps. This will provide your readers with an outline of how your
- plan will be carried out.
- What threats stand in the way and how can they be avoided?
- What mistakes have other businesses made?
- What is the competition doing?
- What is the desired action we want the end user to take?
- What new technology is coming?
- What is your unique perspective and position?
- What is your story?
- Explain what you think is the best route to get there.
- Show an accurate and complete understanding of the client's needs,

especially what is of greatest concern to the client.
- Present a practical plan that responds to the client's greatest concern.
- Focus on an approach that emphasizes the advantages your proposal has to offer.
- Prove that you can be depended on to carry out the plan.
- Describe "how" you will complete steps
- Explain "why" you will complete steps.

Ask these five strategic questions:
1. "What are our broad aspirations for the organization and the concrete goals against which we can measure our progress?
2. Across the potential field available to us, where will we choose to play and not play?
3. In our chosen place to play, how will we choose to win against the competitors there?
4. What capabilities are necessary to build and maintain to win in our chosen manner?
5. What management systems are necessary to operate to build and maintain the key capabilities?

Five Questions to Build a Strategy by Roger Martin May 26, 2010

HOW LONG SHOULD THIS SECTION BE?
This section should be between one paragraph to one page. If you are designing for several user segments, define each group in a separate paragraph.

I THINK THAT, FOR GRADUATING STUDENTS, BREAKING IN IS THE MOST DIFFICULT MOMENT OF THEIR CAREER BECAUSE THEY ARE EMERGING INTO AN OCEAN THAT IS OVERSTOCKED WITH GRADUATE DESIGNERS

ONE OF THE THINGS I TELL STUDENTS WHO ASK ME, "WELL, HOW CAN I GET A JOB?", IS BE REALLY, REALLY GOOD AT ONE THING

DICK POWELL
Partner SeymourPowell UK Industrial design consultancy

Design strategy can involve:
1. Promoting the adoption of a technology
2. Identifying the most important questions that a company's products and services should address
3. Translating insights into actionable solutions
4. Prioritizing the order in which products and services should be launched
5. Connecting design efforts to a business strategy
6. Integrating design as a fundamental aspect of strategic brand intent

EXAMPLE OF A DESIGN STRATEGY
Tom Hardy, Design Strategist, developed the core brand-design principle

"Balance of Reason & Feeling"

for Samsung Electronics, together with rational and emotional attributes, to guide design language within a comprehensive brand-design program that inspired differentiation and elevated the company's global image.

Source: Chung, K.; Freeze, K., "Design Strategy at Samsung Electronics: Becoming a Top-Tier Company, Design Management Institute Case Study - Harvard Business School Publishing, 2008

WHAT IS YOUR UNIQUE VALUE PROPOSITION?

Even the location of your office can be a value proposition.

- Proximity to the client's location may result in improved communications.
- Reduced transportation, travel, and communications expense.
- Proximity to materials and equipment may offer a cost and scheduling advantage.
- If these advantages are significant say so in your proposal.

IN THIS SECTION

A unique value proposition is a clear statement that describes the benefit of your intended design, how you will solve the customer's and client's needs and what distinguishes you from the competition.

A well known potential client probably is approached by dozens of design companies. There needs to be something that makes you special in order for them to slect yopur company.

A value proposition is a statement of how your product or service will benefit your customer. It clearly defines what you will do for your ideal customer and why you're better than your competitors

- What is the product that you are designing?
- What is the end-benefit of using it?
- Who is your target customer for this product?
- What makes your offering unique and different?

WHAT IS A GOOD VALUE PROPOSITION?
- The reader can understand it easily.
- The benefits that a customer will get from using your products is tangible.
- It defines how it is better than the competitor's offer.
- It avoids hype and jargon.
- It can be read and understood in a few seconds

EXAMPLES OF VALUE PROPOSITIONS

SOME EXAMPLES OF COMPELLING VALUE PROPOSITIONS
- Best quality
- Best value
- Best performance
- Best experience
- Easiest to use
- Greatest luxury

DOLLAR SHAVE CLUB
A great shave for a few bucks a month. No commitment. No fees. No BS.

MIDDEN AND MAIN
Performance fabric. Traditional style.

FRESHBOOKS
Small business software design for you the non accountant

SKYPE
Skype keeps the world talking for free

SPOTIFY
Brings you the right music for every mood and moment. The perfect songs for your workout, your night in, or your journey to work.

WHAT IS A BAD VALUE PROPOSITION?
Being the cheapest is a bad value proposition for a designer. Ultimately you will need to become unprofitable in order to maintain this position.

If there is no definition of meetings in your proposal you will at some time experience the type of client who will spend far too much time in unproductive meetings. I usually specify one three-hou meeting per phase for a fixed charge and add the note that additional meeting time will be charged at our usual hourly rate. If you do not do this you may spend a lot of time in meetings that the client is unwilling to pay for.

SCHEDULE OF CLIENT MEETINGS

Most projects require periodic meetings where the design team and stakeholders get together to discuss the project's goals, tasks, deliverables and progress.

Meet only when there is no other practical way to achieve your aims and keep meetings as brief as possible.

TYPE OF MEETINGS

KICKOFF
The stakeholders meet to discusss logistics, tasks, schedule, roles, communication and deliverables.

PLANNING
Make decisions about how the project will be implemented.

PROBLEM SOLVING
Brainstorm solutions with the team.

PRESENTATIONS
Formal presentations to stakeholders, clients and managers

MILESTONE
Critical points in the project plan when phases are completed.

EXAMPLE OF A SCHEDULE OF CLIENT MEETINGS

WEEK 1: Kickoff meeting

WEEK 3: Review of research

WEEK 5: Synthesis POV Review

WEEK 7: Concept Presentation and Review

WEEK 9: Concept refinement review

WEEK 11: Progress review

WEEK 12: Prototype review

WEEK 14: User testing review

WEEK 15: Database review

WEEK 16: Vendor review

WEEK 20: First sample review

WEEK 22: Launch

GOOD DESIGN

**IS INNOVATIVE
MAKES A PRODUCT USEFUL
IS AESTHETIC
MAKES A PRODUCT UNDERSTANDABLE
IS UNOBTRUSIVE
IS HONEST
IS LONG-LASTING
IS THOROUGH DOWN TO THE LAST DETAIL
IS ENVIRONMENTALLY FRIENDLY
IS AS LITTLE DESIGN AS POSSIBLE**

DIETER RAMS

04
ANATOMY OF A PROPOSAL
DESIGN PHASE DEFINITION

DESIGN PHASE DEFINITION

Any changes which will affect the budget should be approved by the client and signed off on with an authorization to proceed. A request for additional budget can create an unhappy client. A skilled project manager can usually manage a project within budget.

The design process is a series of steps used by designers to create products and services.

In this chapter I have defined some proposal content for typical design phases that apply across design disciplines. Use the content as a guide and adapt it to your particular project requirements. The process is iterative. Tasks sometimes need to be repeated before the next stage can be started.

So how do you estimate a project when you may be venturing into new territory and iterations cannot be foreseen? The designer should base the proposal on a well considered and detailed brief. The proposal is broken down into phases or stages. Provide in your cover letter and in your initial proposal a statement that the proposal is based on available writing at the time of writing. After the first stage is completed review the available information and update the details of the next stage. Obtain the client's approval and authorization to proceed for the revised stage before commencing the next stage. Diligence in scoping the project is the designer's responsibility so take care to ask all of the important questions when formulating the original brief. You may find it helpful to review the questions in the briefing checklist in this book when formulating your original proposal.

Design phase definition 101

This section is the core of your proposal. In this section of your proposal you will define each of your design phases and in each phase define the tasks deliverables, phase objectives, phase description and summarize extimated costs, hours worked and phase duration.

The phases that you describe will depend on the particular design project that you are quoting. In this chapter I have provided a template that is commonly used in design companies. I have applied this structure to generic design phases including discovery, synthesis, ideation, and prototyping. The structure can be applied to the particular design phases that you will be undrtaking.

It is important to distinguish between tasks and deliverables. A task is what you do when you design something and a deliverable is what you deliver to the client. Tasks are verbs. Deliverables are nouns.

TASKS
The tasks are what the designer does in order to create a deliverable for example, you may do a brainstorming session in order to create a cocept direction. The concept rendering is what you deliver to the client. Th brainstorming session is the task that you undertake to create the concept that is delivered. Some examples of product design tasks are undertake human factors evaluation, explore design concepts, interview research subjects, or to conduct a brainstorming session.

DELIVERABLES
Deliverable is a term used in project management to describe a tangible or intangible product or service produced as a result of the project that is intended to be delivered to a client. Some examples of product design deliverables are sketches, prototypes, engineering databases, and research reports.

Allow a fixed time such as three hours for the end-of-phase review meeting. If the time is not defined some clients will ask for several meetings which may cause your project to run over budget. Defining the meeting duration discourages clients from requesting too many meetings beyond what is needed for effective project management and communication.

If additional time is necessary, the time can be quoted when details are known.

TASK TIME ESTIMATES

Times for research tasks will vary widely based on the scope of individual projects. Here are some typical time estimates.
- Preparation for a single project: ten hours
- Recruiting and scheduling: two to three hours per person
- Contextual inquiry/task analysis: five hours per person
- Focus groups: three hours per group
- Usability tests: three hours per participant
- Analysing contextual inquiry/task analysis: five hours per person
- Analysing focus group results: four hours per group
- Analysing usability tests: two hours per person
- Preparing a report for email delivery: twelve hours
- Preparing a one-hour presentation: six hours

Source for time estimates: Mike Kuniavsky

DISCOVERY PHASE

PHASE DESCRIPTION
During this phase we investigate our users needs. We use a variety of research techniques to investigate the user needs and the product context.

PHASE OBJECTIVES
The primary objective of the Discovery Phase is to gain a high-level understanding of the user needs. By the end of this phase we will have an overview of user needs, competitive products and their effectiveness, business context and have a foundation to explore possible design directions.

PHASE TASKS
- Identify the stakeholders.
- Rank stakeholders according to their importance for the success of the project
- Study preliminary ergonomic and human interface
- Explore and evaluate potential materials and manufacturing processes
- Contextual inquiry to uncover problems users have, both with the product and with the tasks
- Conduct face-to-face stakeholder interviews
- Conduct three focus groups, to determine which features are of highest value
- Conduct three focus groups, to determine what users of the competition's products find most valuable, and where those products fail them
- Competitive usability tests to determine strong and weak points in the

A stakeholder is any person that holds a stake, or has a vested interest in a project. Every stakeholder has different needs and goals. Stakeholders are persons, groups or organizations that can affect or be affected by the design. In the case of a medical device for use in a hospital, stakeholders include the patient, doctors, nurses, hospital workers, relatives of patients, and medical insurance organizations. Stakeholders are also people in the design team and client organization.

The concept of stakeholder was first used in 1963 during an internal memorandum at th Stanford Research institute.

Specify as precisely as possible the size and format of each deliverable. A common cause of conflicts between designer and client is the precise form of a deliverable. For example, if you are delivering a report, state the format of the report, the number of pages and what the report will contain in detail in terms of the report sections and structure. If you are delivering a design concept describe precisely how many concepts will be delivered. Describe whether they will be hand sketches, computer renderings or other format. Define the size of the page or the resolution and file format for a digital image.

competitors' products
- To investigate the existing product in detail.
- To investigate competitive or similar products
- Trend research
- Undertake human factors research
- Prepare a research report
- Undertake preliminary research of the component volumes and physical constraints for Ideation Phase exploration
- Work closely with the client

PHASE DELIVERABLES
- Research plan
- Stakeholder map
- Audience definition
- Competitor research analysis
- Expert review report
- User segmentation models
- Value proposition definition
- Research Phase conclusions and recommendations
- Refined Project budget and schedule
- Working with client IP attorney to investigate existing IP is not included but can be quoted once details are known

PHASE REVIEW MEETING
A review will be held at the designer's facility to discuss the phase deliverables. We have allowed up to three hours for this meeting. If the meeting takes longer than three hours the additional time will be charged as required on an hourly basis when details are known. This meeting will conclude the Discovery Phase.

RESEARCH METHODS

There are hundreds of different research methods that can be used during the Discovery Phase.

I suggest using a mixed methods approach that involves both qualitative and quantitative methods with a minimum sample size of five or six subjects. It is important that you leave your studio and immerse yourself in the user context and engage users.

Some common design research methods are
- Participant-observation
- User interviews
- Focus groups
- Web analytics
- Literature review
- Competitor analysis

DISCOVERY PHASE			
Activity	Hours	Elapsed	Fee
Tasks and deliverables	24.00	2 weeks	$ 4200.00
Meetings	3.00		525.00
		TOTAL	$ 4725.00

Many design companies summarize the costs, hours worked and stage duration at the end of each design phase description. Design companies sometimes place image related to the content within the proposal to provide more visual interest.

SYNTHESIS PHASE

In this stage we review the research, make connections, uncover insights, filter and distill the data. We make sense of the information gathered during the research phase.

An insight is a fresh point of view based on a deep understanding of the way of thinking and behavior. An insight occurs by mentally connecting two or more things that have not been connected before. These things may be things that many people have seen or experienced but not connected before. A goal of the Synthesis Phase is to build actionable insights

PHASE DESCRIPTION

During the Synthesis Phase the research gathered during the Discovery Phase is analysed and synthesised into a brief with actionable tasks related to new product or service development.

PHASE TASKS

- Analyse the research collected in the Discovery Phase
- Create meanings and models from the data
- Re-frame the problem
- Identify themes or common features among the research data
- Identify actionable insights derived from the research data
- Create between five and nine research themes
- Create a list of actionable user insights.
- Create a hierarchy of user issues to be addressed by the design
- Create a Point of View statement identifying clearly the user group, their unmet need(s) and insights to be addressed in the Ideation Phase.
- Refine the design brief based on discovery research
- Work closely with the client

PHASE DELIVERABLES

- Definition of the system and subsystems
- Define the design intent
- 4 to 6 user personas
- Statement of user needs
- One Point of View statement

- Ten "what if" questions
- User Experience or Customer Journey Map(s)
- User stories
- Storyboard(s)
- Stakeholder Map
- Opportunity Map
- Empathy Map(s)
- SWOT analysis of competitive products
- Hierarchy of top 5 to 9 customer pain points
- Hierarchy of 5 to 9 top customer unmet needs.
- Hierarchy of top 5 to 9 design opportunities
- Risk analysis
- SMART design goals
- Refined design brief

PHASE REVIEW MEETING
A review will be held at the designer's facility to discuss the phase deliverables. We have allowed up to three hours for this meeting. If the meeting takes longer than three hours the additional time will be charged as required on an hourly basis when details are known. This meeting will conclude the Synthesis Phase.

The user need statement is the desires or needs of end users expressed in their own words.

A point-of-view (POV) is reframing of a design challenge into an actionable problem statement. The POV is used as the basis for design ideation. The POV defines the design intent. The POV helps re-frame the design problem into an actionable focus for the generation of ideas.

SYNTHESIS PHASE			
Activity	Hours	Elapsed	Fee
Tasks and deliverables	24.00	2 weeks	$ 4200.00
Meetings	3.00		525.00
		TOTAL	$ 4725.00

IDEATION PHASE

PHASE DESCRIPTION
The design firm will explore design concept directions based on the client project goals and user needs with due consideration of product function, use, performance, utility, context of use, interface, maintenance, appearance, materials process and client business goals. and to select a preferred design direction or directions for prototyping and testing with internal and external stakeholders.

PHASE OBJECTIVE
The objective of this phase is explore a wide variety of possible concept directions and to select a number of preferred concept directions for prototyping and stakeholder feedback testing.

PHASE TASKS
- Explore concept directions and design features
- Team brainstorming
- Consider brand signature elements
- Consider user need, usability, and human factors requirements
- Consider business opportunities
- Consider user context
- Consider product/service system
- Individual designer ideation
- Explore a number of alternative materials, finishes and processes
- Explore a number of alternative visual directions
- Explore performance requirements
- Establish general configuration parameters
- Client liaison. Work closely with the client

Between one hundred and one hundred and twenty fast concept ideas is a good body of design exploration for the majority of industrial design projects in order to select one viable direction for prototyping and testing with stakeholders.

The core areas of exploration should be
1. The business requirements
2. The user needs
3. The technology, process and material requirements

The best results for exploration are generated by a team of between four and twelve cross disciplinary professionals. A diverse team of different genders, occupations ages, cultural backgrounds is preferred.

PHASE DELIVERABLES

- 80 to 120 concept sketches of alternative design directions highlighting a range of workable product solutions
- 4 to 6 color product renderings of preferred concept design directions (specify the format and size of the renderings in as much detail as possible, for example: "Two variations of each of three concept directions, presented as 300 dpi 3D view color renderings, each 8.5 inch x 11.0 inch. Total of six color renderings"
- Manufacturing strategy(s)
- Low fidelity prototype(s)

PHASE MEETINGS

A review will be held at the designer's facility to discuss the phase deliverables. The goal of this meeting will be to select four six preferred design directions for prototyping and testing. We have allowed up to three hours for this meeting. If the meeting takes longer than three hours the additional time will be charged as required on an hourly basis when details are known. This meeting will conclude the Ideation Phase.

It is best that the end users are involved in the selection of the preferred design direction. Studies show that over 75% of new products fail in the market. The primary reason that new products fail in the market is a lack of awareness of the customer's point of view. My preference is that four to six concept directions are selected in the review meeting for the Ideation Phase and that these are prototyped and tested with end users before selecting a single preferred concept direction.

IDEATION PHASE

Activity	Hours	Elapsed	Fee
Tasks and deliverables	24.00	2 weeks	$ 4200.00
Meetings	3.00		525.00
		TOTAL	$ 4725.00

LOW FIDELITY PROTOTYPE CONSTRUCTION PHASE

The testing process of the low fidelity prototype is more important as a deliverable than the physical prototype.

Low fidelity prototypes are constructed at maximum speed and minimum cost to test the performance, usability and features of a proposed design with project stakeholders.

Aim for fidelity of the experience and not of the prototype.

PHASE DESCRIPTION
In this phase the design will be prototyped at maximum speed and minimum cost so that the usability and performance of the proposed design can be evaluated with stakeholders.

OBJECTIVE
To construct one or several low fidelity prototypes of the perspective product;- to serve as a basis for testing and evaluating its functional performance and check product features, and usability. The prototype(s) will be refined through iterative stages of field testing and user feedback to incorporate input from stakeholders, prior to production.

PHASE TASKS
- Construct representative prototype(s) of the proposed design.

PHASE DELIVERABLES
- Low fidelity prototype(s) of the proposed design.
- It is assumed for the purpose of this proposal that one prototype will be constructed and that there will be three iterations of testing and refinement. If more prototypes and iterations of testing are necessary these can be quoted prior to construction and testing.
- These prototypes will be constructed to test features and usability of the proposed design. The prototype(s) will function for stakeholder feedback like the proposed design but not have the appearance of the final design.

PHASE MEETINGS

A review will be held at the designer's facility to discuss the phase deliverables. We have allowed up to three hours for this meeting. If the meeting takes longer than three hours the additional time will be charged as required on an hourly basis when details are known. This meeting will conclude the Low Fidelity Prototype construction Phase.

When quoting stages that have a higher level of uncertainty indicate in the initial proposal that these stages can be defined prior to implementation when details are known. Create a change order when you reach that point in the project and obtain the client approval prior to implementation.

LOW-FIDELITY PROTOTYPE			
Activity	Hours	Elapsed	Fee
Tasks and deliverables	24.00	2 weeks	$ 4200.00
Meetings	3.00		525.00
		TOTAL	$ 4725.00

USABILITY TESTING

- Test proposed design
- Test competitor's designs
- Test in the real context of use
- Test iteratively
- Use heuristics and usability guidelines
- Test at least five people from each user group.

PHASE DESCRIPTION
Usability testing is a technique used in user-centered interaction design to evaluate a product by testing it on users. Usability testing focuses on measuring a design's fitness for an intended purpose. Usability testing involves observation under controlled conditions to determine how people use the design and how the design might be improved.

Real users undertake particular tasks. Researchers and other stakeholders observe and collect data.

OBJECTIVE
Usability testing helps improve a design to make it more usable.

PHASE TASKS
- Develop a test plan
- Choose a testing space
- Recruit participants
- Prepare test materials
- Conduct the tests
- Debrief participants
- Analyze data
- Problems experienced by the test user will be identified through testing and observation
- The prototype will be refined to fix the problems
- The testing and feedback process will be undertaken in iterative cycles until all design problems are resolved

PHASE DELIVERABLES
- A usability testing report with design conclusions and recommendations based on customer feedback
- A refined design with impoved usability

PHASE MEETINGS
A review will be held at the designer's facility to discuss the phase deliverables. We have allowed up to three hours for this meeting. If the meeting takes longer than three hours the additional time will be charged as required on an hourly basis when details are known. This meeting will conclude the Usability Testing Phase.

DIAGNOSTIC EVALUATION
1. Test 4-6 users
2. Find and fix problems
3. During design development
4. Test iteratively

SUMMATIVE TESTING
1. How many? 6-12 users
2. Metrics based on usability goals
3. Test to measure the success of a design.
4. When At end of process
5. Test once

USABILITY TESTING PHASE			
Activity	Hours	Elapsed	Fee
Tasks and deliverables	24.00	2 weeks	$ 4200.00
Meetings	3.00		525.00
		TOTAL	$ 4725.00

FURTHER STAGES

In the previous pages I have illustrated a model that can be applied to your project. In my experience every project requires some customization of the phase descriptions, tasks and deliverables. This approach can be used across different design disciplines for time and materials proposals.

ENGINEERING DATABASE

PHASE DESCRIPTION

Lorem ipsum dolor sit amet, consectetur adipiscing elit. Praesent sagittis, metus sed porta commodo, tortor magna mollis eros, quis elementum mi metus vitae purus. Etiam luctus scelerisque nisi, vitae scelerisque tortor maximus eget. Nulla in tincidunt felis. Donec ut lacinia metus, sit amet.

PHASE TASKS

- Lorem ipsum dolor sit amet, consectetur adipiscing elit.
- Praesent sagittis, metus sed porta commodo, tortor magna mollis eros, quis elementum mi metus vitae purus.
- Etiam luctus scelerisque nisi, vitae scelerisque tortor maximus eget. Nulla in tincidunt felis.

PHASE DELIVERABLES

- Praesent sagittis, metus sed porta commodo, tortor magna mollis eros, quis elementum mi metus vitae purus.
- Etiam luctus scelerisque nisi, vitae scelerisque tortor maximus eget. Nulla in tincidunt felis.
- Donec ut lacinia metus, sit amet ultricies nisl. Cras ut libero nulla. Pellentesque iaculis congue porta.

PHASE MEETINGS

Lorem ipsum dolor sit amet, consectetur adipiscing elit. Praesent sagittis, metus sed porta commodo, tortor magna mollis eros, quis elementum mi metus vitae purus. Etiam luctus scelerisque nisi, vitae scelerisque tortor maximus eget.

ENGINEERING DATABASE			
Activity	Hours	Elapsed	Fee
Tasks and deliverables	24.00	2 weeks	$ 4200.00
Meetings	3.00		525.00
		TOTAL	$ 4725.00

FURTHER STAGES

In the previous pages I have illustrated a model that can be applied to your project. In my experience every project requires some customization of the phase descriptions, tasks and deliverables. This approach can be used across different design disciplines for time and materials proposals.

IMPLEMENTATION PHASE

PHASE DESCRIPTION
Lorem ipsum dolor sit amet, consectetur adipiscing elit. Praesent sagittis, metus sed porta commodo, tortor magna mollis eros, quis elementum mi metus vitae purus. Etiam luctus scelerisque nisi, vitae scelerisque tortor maximus eget. Nulla in tincidunt felis. Donec ut lacinia metus, sit amet.

PHASE TASKS
- Lorem ipsum dolor sit amet, consectetur adipiscing elit.
- Praesent sagittis, metus sed porta commodo, tortor magna mollis eros, quis elementum mi metus vitae purus.
- Etiam luctus scelerisque nisi, vitae scelerisque tortor maximus eget. Nulla in tincidunt felis.

PHASE DELIVERABLES
- Praesent sagittis, metus sed porta commodo, tortor magna mollis eros, quis elementum mi metus vitae purus.
- Etiam luctus scelerisque nisi, vitae scelerisque tortor maximus eget. Nulla in tincidunt felis.
- Donec ut lacinia metus, sit amet ultricies nisl. Cras ut libero nulla. Pellentesque iaculis congue porta.

PHASE MEETINGS
Lorem ipsum dolor sit amet, consectetur adipiscing elit. Praesent sagittis, metus sed porta commodo, tortor magna mollis eros, quis elementum mi metus vitae purus. Etiam luctus scelerisque nisi, vitae scelerisque tortor maximus eget.

DISCOVERY PHASE

Activity	Hours	Elapsed	Fee
Tasks and deliverables	24.00	2 weeks	$ 4200.00
Meetings	3.00		525.00
		TOTAL	$ 4725.00

GRAPHICS PROGRAM

PHASE DESCRIPTION
Lorem ipsum dolor sit amet, consectetur adipiscing elit. Praesent sagittis, metus sed porta commodo, tortor magna mollis eros, quis elementum mi metus vitae purus. Etiam luctus scelerisque nisi, vitae scelerisque tortor maximus eget. Nulla in tincidunt felis. Donec ut lacinia metus, sit amet.

PHASE TASKS
- Lorem ipsum dolor sit amet, consectetur adipiscing elit.
- Praesent sagittis, metus sed porta commodo, tortor magna mollis eros, quis elementum mi metus vitae purus.
- Etiam luctus scelerisque nisi, vitae scelerisque tortor maximus eget. Nulla in tincidunt felis.

PHASE DELIVERABLES
- Praesent sagittis, metus sed porta commodo, tortor magna mollis eros, quis elementum mi metus vitae purus.
- Etiam luctus scelerisque nisi, vitae scelerisque tortor maximus eget. Nulla in tincidunt felis.
- Donec ut lacinia metus, sit amet ultricies nisl. Cras ut libero nulla. Pellentesque iaculis congue porta.

PHASE MEETINGS
Lorem ipsum dolor sit amet, consectetur adipiscing elit. Praesent sagittis, metus sed porta commodo, tortor magna mollis eros, quis elementum mi metus vitae purus. Etiam luctus scelerisque nisi, vitae scelerisque tortor maximus eget.

DISCOVERY PHASE

Activity	Hours	Elapsed	Fee
Tasks and deliverables	24.00	2 weeks	$ 4200.00
Meetings	3.00		525.00
		TOTAL	$ 4725.00

MATERIALS & FINISHES PROGRAM

PHASE DESCRIPTION
Lorem ipsum dolor sit amet, consectetur adipiscing elit. Praesent sagittis, metus sed porta commodo, tortor magna mollis eros, quis elementum mi metus vitae purus. Etiam luctus scelerisque nisi, vitae scelerisque tortor maximus eget. Nulla in tincidunt felis. Donec ut lacinia metus, sit amet.

PHASE TASKS
- Lorem ipsum dolor sit amet, consectetur adipiscing elit.
- Praesent sagittis, metus sed porta commodo, tortor magna mollis eros, quis elementum mi metus vitae purus.
- Etiam luctus scelerisque nisi, vitae scelerisque tortor maximus eget. Nulla in tincidunt felis.

PHASE DELIVERABLES
- Praesent sagittis, metus sed porta commodo, tortor magna mollis eros, quis elementum mi metus vitae purus.
- Etiam luctus scelerisque nisi, vitae scelerisque tortor maximus eget. Nulla in tincidunt felis.
- Donec ut lacinia metus, sit amet ultricies nisl. Cras ut libero nulla. Pellentesque iaculis congue porta.

PHASE MEETINGS
Lorem ipsum dolor sit amet, consectetur adipiscing elit. Praesent sagittis, metus sed porta commodo, tortor magna mollis eros, quis elementum mi metus vitae purus. Etiam luctus scelerisque nisi, vitae scelerisque tortor maximus eget.

DISCOVERY PHASE

Activity	Hours	Elapsed	Fee
Tasks and deliverables	24.00	2 weeks	$ 4200.00
Meetings	3.00		525.00
		TOTAL	$ 4725.00

SOURCING PROGRAM

PHASE DESCRIPTION
Lorem ipsum dolor sit amet, consectetur adipiscing elit. Praesent sagittis, metus sed porta commodo, tortor magna mollis eros, quis elementum mi metus vitae purus. Etiam luctus scelerisque nisi, vitae scelerisque tortor maximus eget. Nulla in tincidunt felis. Donec ut lacinia metus, sit amet.

PHASE TASKS
- Lorem ipsum dolor sit amet, consectetur adipiscing elit.
- Praesent sagittis, metus sed porta commodo, tortor magna mollis eros, quis elementum mi metus vitae purus.
- Etiam luctus scelerisque nisi, vitae scelerisque tortor maximus eget. Nulla in tincidunt felis.

PHASE DELIVERABLES
- Praesent sagittis, metus sed porta commodo, tortor magna mollis eros, quis elementum mi metus vitae purus.
- Etiam luctus scelerisque nisi, vitae scelerisque tortor maximus eget. Nulla in tincidunt felis.
- Donec ut lacinia metus, sit amet ultricies nisl. Cras ut libero nulla. Pellentesque iaculis congue porta.

PHASE MEETINGS
Lorem ipsum dolor sit amet, consectetur adipiscing elit. Praesent sagittis, metus sed porta commodo, tortor magna mollis eros, quis elementum mi metus vitae purus. Etiam luctus scelerisque nisi, vitae scelerisque tortor maximus eget.

DISCOVERY PHASE

Activity	Hours	Elapsed	Fee
Tasks and deliverables	24.00	2 weeks	$ 4200.00
Meetings	3.00		525.00
		TOTAL	$ 4725.00

AUTHORIZATION TO PROCEED

IN THIS SECTION
The authorization to proceed is one of the most important pages in a design proposal. You should never start work on a design project before receiving a signed authorisation to proceed. Do not accept an assurance that it will be signed. It is the legal contract between designer and client and the signatures indicate that client has read the proposal and accepts it legally. If you do not get paid then this is the document that you will use in court to enforce your right to be paid. Make sure that the person representing your client is legally entitled to sign on behalf of the client organization. That is usually a CEO or member of the board of directors. Many companies accept digital signature using online authorization systems such as the one offered by Adobe in order to speed up the process. Exchanging contracts by mail can slow the start of a project by several weeks.

HOW LONG SHOULD THIS SECTION BE?
It is usually one page and is often located after the page outlining the summary of fees in a proposal.

EXAMPLE OF AN AUTHORIZATION TO PROCEED

To initiate the design program the designer requires a purchase order deposit and signed authorization to proceed. This document is to confirm that the Designer has authorization to proceed as outlined in:

PROPOSAL NUMBER

PROPOSAL VERSION NUMBER

DATE

PROPOSAL NUMBER

DESCRIPTION OF SERVICES

DEPOSIT	**TOTAL VALUE OF AUTHORIZED STAGES**

The person signing this agreement on behalf of each organization below acknowleges that he or she is binding the entire company or entity and represents that he or she has authority to do so. The designer will commence work upon receipt of this form.

PROPOSAL AND TERMS ACCEPTED BY CLIENT

....
Print Name & Title   Signature   Date

PROPOSAL AND TERMS ACCEPTED BY DESIGNER

....
Print Name & Title   Signature   Date

SUMMARY OF FEES

Your proposal will probably be passed on to a client diector for approval. They are often busy people. The information that most interests them are the executive summary and the fee schedule pages. The person approving your proposal may only read those two pages.

I usually include the hous worked as well as the elapsed time for each stage. Later stages I often include as "TBD" of "To Be Determined" if the briefing information is insufficient to determine a reliable estimate for that stage. The client wants to see as many stages quoted as possible. Be sure to use the heading estimate. Almost always there are differences of scope between what is quoted in early stages and what the client requests to be delivered. A good project manager will control scope creep.

EXAMPLE OF SUMMARY OF FEES

FEE ESTIMATE			
Activity	Hours	Elapsed	Fee
Discovery Phase	400.00	4 weeks	$ 60000.00
Meeting	3.00		450.00
Synthesis Phase	80.00	2 weeks	12000.00
Meeting	3.00		450.00
Ideation Phase	240.00	3 weeks	36000.00
Meeting	3.00		450.00
Preliminary Engineering Database	80.00	2 weeks	12000.00
Meeting	3.00		450.00
Prototype Phase	60.00	2 weeks	9000.00
Meeting	3.00		450.00
Testing Phase	TBD	TBD	TBD
Meeting	TBD	TBD	TBD
Implementation Phase	TBD	TBD	TBD
Meeting	TBD	TBD	TBD
TOTAL FOR QUOTED PHASES	875.00	13 weeks	130800.00

REIMBURESMENTS

This page is not always included in a time and materials proposal. The client may request a not-to-exceed amount for reimburesements based on your estimate in order to get internal approval for the project budget in their organization. The client may request a berak down of estimates for reimbursements ina table such as the example that I have provided here. It is common not to define reimburesements in the proposal but to bill them on an as required basis each month with a breakdown in the invoice supplied to the client. Sometimes a client will request that reimburesements do not exceed a percentage of the overall project budget which may be 10% or 20%.

Design phase definition 123

REIMBURESMENTS

REIMBURSEMENTS			
Activity	Cost	Number	Subtotal
Copies			
Prints			
Courier services			
Fabrication			
Legal fees			
Model making			
Photography			
Photographic prints			
Rapid prototypes			
Portable media			
Scanning			
Research materials			
Travel			
Meals			
Post-it-notes			
Other			
		TOTAL	

GANTT CHART SCHEDULE

WHAT IS IT?
A Gantt chart is a bar chart that shows the tasks of a project, the start time and the time from start to completion of each task.

This method is used widely in industry to ensure that activities are completed on time and on budget.

WHO INVENTED IT?
Henry Gantt first published in "Organizing for Work 1919.

WHY USE THIS METHOD?
1. Use to track a design project
2. Use to ensure that tasks are completed on time.

HOW TO USE THIS METHOD
1. Identify the tasks
2. Identify the milestones in the project.
3. Identify the time required for each task.
4. Identify the order and dependencies of each task.
5. Identify the tasks that can be undertaken in parallel
6. Draw a horizontal time axis along the top or bottom of a page.
7. Draw a list of tasks in order down the left hand side of the page in the order that they should be undertaken.
8. Draw a diamond for tasks that are short in duration such as a meeting
9. For longer activities draw a horizontal bar indicating the planned duration.

EXAMPLE OF A PROJECT SCHEDULE

This example is created in a spread sheet. There are may good project management programs that can create gantt charts based on your input of data. One very widely used progam is Microsoft Project. Thse programs allow you to adjust resources in a dynamic way as required and to update the schedule chart if for example someone leaves or is sick or if you need to move human resources from one project to another.

SCHEDULE GANTT CHART

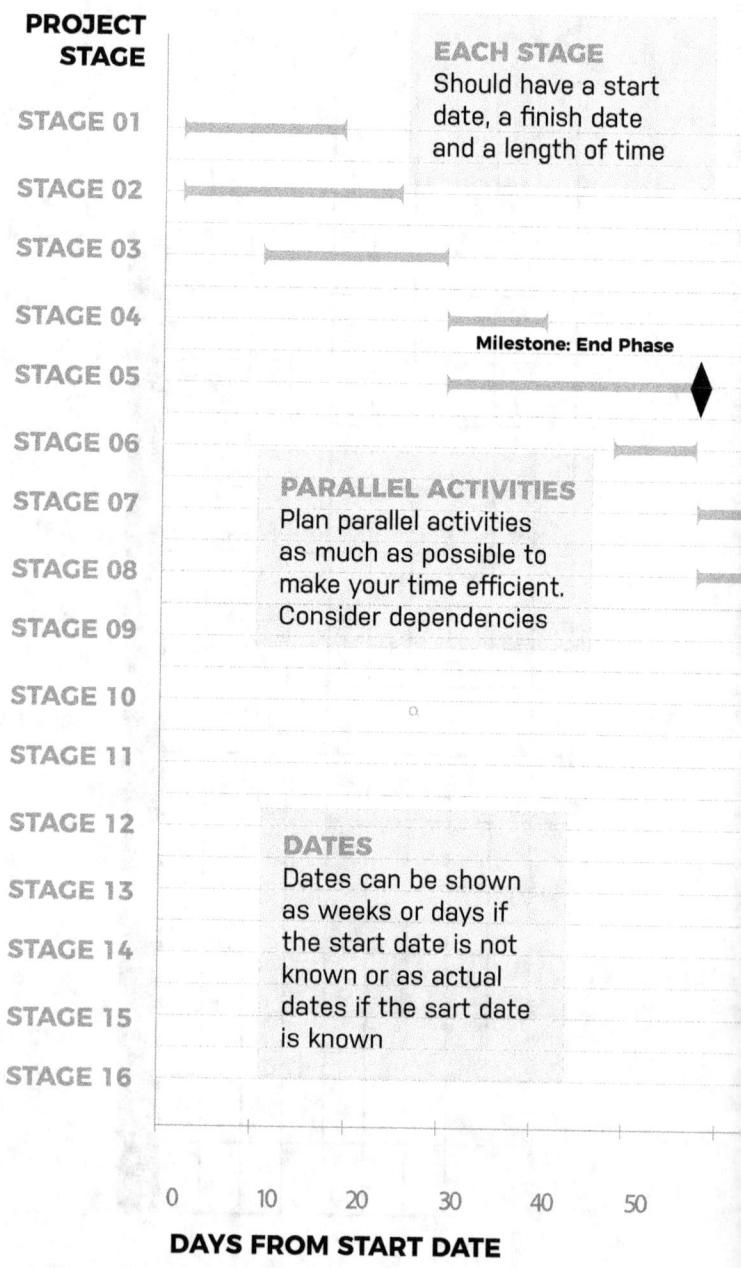

Design phase definition 127

COLOR
Use color to show different phases

STAGES
Break the project into major components then tasks and subtasks

MILESTONES
Choose a symbol to represent milestones, that is, major events that either have a large part in the process or must be completed before progress can continue. Name the milestones

Milestone: Deliver Prototype

RESOURCES
Consider the people you will have available, other projects, holidays and weekends when people may not be working

Milestone: End Phase

90 100 100 120 130 140 150 160

EXAMPLE OF OF STAGES FOR A PRODUCT SMALL PROJECT

1. Preliminary research
2. Research elderly
3. Research competitors
4. Interview experts
5. Interview external stakeholders
6. Interview internal stakeholders
7. Observe stakeholders
8. Focus groups
9. Research review
10. Synthesis
11. Point of view statement
12. Concept origination
13. Initiate color materials and finish program
14. Initiate product graphics program
15. Brainstorming/Clustering
16. Design review
17. IP review for prior art
18. Refine concepts
19. Build preliminary engineering database
20. Build low-fidelity prototypes
21. Stakeholder testing
22. Analysis of testing
23. Produce report
24. Design review
25. Refine engineering database
26. Source production vendors
27. Build high-fidelity prototype
28. Stakeholder testing
29. Analysis of testing
30. Produce report
31. Design review
32. Refine concepts
33. Refine engineering database
34. Select production vendors
35. Tooling
36. Freliminary production
37. First sample review
38. Refine engineering database

EXAMPLE OF STAGES
FOR A PRODUCT LARGE PROJECT

1. Market Overview
2. Assumptions
3. Financials
4. Product Overview
5. Strategic Fit
6. Market Assessment
7. Project Plan
8. Risks
9. Questions
10. Recommendation
11. Opportunity Statement: Marketing
12. Market Overview
13. Assumptions
14. Financials
15. Product Overview
16. Strategic Fit
17. Market Assessment
18. Project Plan
19. Risks
20. Questions
21. Recommendation
22. List of Competing Products with details
23. SWOT of all Competing Products
24. Customer Journey Map
25. Competitior Profiling
26. Media Profiling
27. Key Success Factors
28. Competitor Rating
29. P&L Projections
30. Cash-flow projections
31. Capital Expenditures
32. Operating Expenses
33. Break-even analysis
34. Identify external and Internal resources
35. Estimate resource requirement
36. Obtain Internal funding approval
37. Brief designer
38. Initiate project Management
39. Create schedule
40. Identify team
41. Preliminary research
42. Research elderly
43. Research competitors
44. Interview experts
45. Interview external stakeholders
46. Interview internal stakeholders
47. Observe stakeholders
48. Focus groups
49. Research review
50. Synthesis
51. ID Concept Origination
52. Generate Concept Sketches
53. Foam and card Scale Models
54. Brief Patent Attorney
55. Patent Search Patent Attorney
56. Select Favored Concept Direction
57. Concept Refinement
58. Refined Sketch Concepts
59. Full size foam and Card models
60. Computer Illustrations 5 Directions
61. Non Structural Visual Models
62. Concept Review
63. Prototype One Documentation
64. Review Refinements to Design
65. Produce 3D Assembly of Prototype
66. Review with Modelmakers
67. Review of CAD Assembly
68. Individual Dimensioned Part
69. Documentation/ Refinements to design
70. Brief Modelmakers
71. Designers Ineteract with Modelmakers and provide further definition during construction
72. Prototype Construction
73. Prototype Review
74. Prototype Two Documentation
75. Review Refinements to Design
76. Produce 3D Assembly of Prototype

77. Review with Model-makers
78. Review of CAD Assembly
79. Prototype Individual Dimensioned Part Documentation
80. Refinements to design
81. Brief Model-makers
82. Designers Interact with Model-makers and provide further definition during construction
83. Prototype Two Construction
84. Review
85. Color Finish and Materials Development:
86. Marketing Opportunity Statement/ Competitive evaluation
87. Material Soucing
88. Concepts
89. Review
90. Concept Refinement
91. Review
92. Prototype One
93. Review
94. Refinements
95. Review
96. Prototype Two
97. Review Refinements
98. Production Definition
99. Group meeting
100. Human Factors Evaluation
101. Ergonomist reviews selected design direction
102. Ergonomist recommends to design team critical ergonomic considerations
103. Ergonomist sources relevant human factors standards and supplies design team with copies
104. Ergonomist review of prototype with team
105. Ergonomist produces recommended design refinements
106. Review
107. obtain samples existing parts
108. Determine Internal or external development
109. Raise Order
110. Color definition
111. Testing
112. Customer Validation
113. Protype Two
114. Review
115. Design Refinements
116. Engineering Refinements
117. Testing
118. Customer Validation
119. Design Freeze
120. 126Privacy screen development
121. Identify 3 consultancies
122. Obtain consultancy costings
123. Design Concepts
124. Level 3 Review
125. Concept Refinement
126. Level 2 review
127. Select favored concept
128. Engineering Specification of Parts
129. Prototype One
130. Level One Review
131. Design Refinements
132. Engineering Refinements
133. Color definition
134. Testing
135. Customer Validation
136. Protype Two
137. Design Refinements
138. Engineering Refinements
139. Testing
140. Customer Validation
141. Reccommendations
142. Design Modifications
143. Engineering Modifications
144. Material and Finish Modifications
145. Prototype Two
146. Design Modifications
147. Engineering Modifications
148. 175Material and Finish Modifications

Design phase definition 131

149. Patent attorney Investigation
150. Visual Mock Up
151. Level 2, 3, and 4 Reviews
152. Design Refinements In conjunction with desk tool definitions
153. Engineering Refinements
154. Finish Refinements
155. Extrusion Tooling
156. Off Tool Samples
157. Prototype Two
158. Level 1, 2, 3 and 4 Reviews
159. Testing with
160. Recruit survey participanys from area managers
161. Recruit participants,
162. Create Survey, Create Cover Invitation, Arrange for travel and participant payment, Recruite Experts
163. Design Direction evaluated and documented
164. Discussion Guide
165. Interviews
166. Team briefing
167. Launch Envisioning Exercise

THERE ARE NO CLIENT CONFLICTS, ONLY BAD EXPLANATIONS

JERRY DELLA FEMINA
American advertising executive and restaurateur

05
ANATOMY OF A PROPOSAL
END SECTIONS OF A PROPOSAL

MY TASK, WHICH I AM TRYING TO ACHIEVE IS, BY THE POWER OF THE WRITTEN WORD, TO MAKE YOU HEAR, TO MAKE YOU FEEL, IT IS, BEFORE ALL, TO MAKE YOU SEE

JOSEPH CONRAD
Polish-British writer

END SECTIONS OF A PROPOSAL

After your definitions of design phases you create sections of the proposal.

1. Conclusion
2. Next steps
3. Company overview
4. Awards
5. Team
6. Clients
7. Case studies
8. Additional services
9. Terms & conditions

The proposal sections provide evidence for the client that you have the knowlege and skills to undertake the project successfully. You have the qualified team, related project experience, the resources and recognition from your peers in the form of industry awards that are a winning combination.

Terms and conditions are an essential part of the proposal. These are sometimes located after the fee structure page.

CONCLUSION

1. Will the client benefit from a summary of your main points?
2. Can you identify a main point that would give it added weight?
3. What larger principle stands behind the main point?
4. Why is the main point significant?

IN THIS SECTION
This section of the proposal is most concerned with the bigger picture. The conclusion should recap what the designer intends to do. The conclusion should bring closure to the many points discussed in the body of the proposal. The conclusion should help the reader understand the significance of the issues being proposed.

A proposal conclusion calls for action from the client and summarizes the benefits of this action. In some proposals the conclusion calls for more research or resolution before a decision can be made by the client. Most commonly the conclusion is a summary of the issues being discussed in the body of the proposal. This is most important in a long or complex proposal.

The conclusion may be the only section of a proposal that is read by a CEO and so should be a convincing call to action. The conclusion can provide a hook to bring the reader back to an important idea in the introduction.

HOW LONG SHOULD THIS SECTION BE?
This section should be between one paragraph to one page.

EXAMPLE OF A CONCLUSION

Axis Design Firm bids $28,000 to design a computer desk for use in Californian Schools. The objective is to aid school children between the ages of ten and fourteen years to develop better reading skills. The design will be flexible and allow for future educational needs by a unique patented connection logic. The desk will provide a unique platform for quantifying learner performance in developing spelling skills through a tablet based cloud system.

The desk will be developed over seven weeks. We will start the project within seven days of receiving your official order, the signed authorization to proceed contained in this proposal and the and project deposit of $14,000.

Axis is uniquely qualified to design this product based on our experience developing three similar products for Education LLC over a period of ten years that currently hold sixty percent of the education market in California.

EXAMPLE OF NEXT STEPS

In this section Close the proposal with a convincing call to action. Leave no doubt as to what their next steps should be. This section lets a client know exactly what they need to do to start a project. It should be simple and understandable.

How long should this section be? This section should be between one paragraph to half a page.

Axis design firm are excited to work with you to bring this project to reality.

To initiate this proposal return to to the address below an original copy of the signed Authorization to Proceed that you can find on page 14 of this proposal before June 12th with your official company order for the amount of $28,000 and the project first phase deposit of $14,000.

Please contact me if you need any more information.

Thank you for the opportunity to provide our proposal to work with you to bring this project to success.

Tom Brithtson
Partner
Axis Design LLC
14 Tech Center Road
Topanga CA 90290.
E-mail tbrithtson@axis.com
Phone 316-246-8184

EXAMPLE OF NEXT STEPS

To proceed with this project, take the following steps:

1. Accept the proposal as is or discuss desired changes.
2. Finalize and e-sign this authorization to proceed
3. Email me your official company order for the amount of $10,000
4. Provide the phase one deposit of $5,000 via PayPal to email:adesigner@abc.com
5. Once paid, I'll begin production Monday, July 22, 2025 for a deadline of Monday, August 6, 2025.

Thank You

Please contact me if you need any more information. I appreciate the opportunity to send you this proposal for your project. Upon receipt of the above we will email your payment invoice. I look forward to working with you to make this project a success!

Tom Brithtson
Partner
Axis Design LLC
14 Tech Center Road
Topanga CA 90290.
E-mail tbrithtson@axis.com
Phone 316-246-8184

COMPANY OVERVIEW

IN THIS SECTION
A company overview is an essential part of a business plan. A good company description should include: the nature of your business and the needs it aims to fulfil. Detail what your services are. Define your business' legal status, such as whether you are a partnership, sole proprietary or corporate business. Make your unique values and competitive advantages clear.

This section should be a simple honest and authentic summary of your design organization highlighting those things that demonstrate that you are a good fit for the client. Answer the questions "who, what, when, where, and why" of your business.

WHO IS YOUR INTENDED AUDIENCE?
Consider the perspective of your audience. They want to know about what you can do for them. Include the things everyone should know about you. Don't make the assumption that the client knows who you are. Support your claims with quantifiable evidence where possible.

HOW LONG SHOULD THIS SECTION BE?
Keep your company overview to no more than one page and keep it up to date.

WHERE SHOULD THIS SECTION BE?
The company overview is sometimes placed in the leading sections of the proposal and sometimes in the end sections of the proposal with the team and case studies. Place it in the leading sections if you are working with a new client who doesn't know your organization.

EXAMPLE OF A COMPANY OVERVIEW

Axis Design is an international design innovation consultancy. For 20 years Axis has been improving people's lives through human-centered design. We partner with leaders in the private and public sectors to design and implement:

- Products
- Services
- Brand
- Digital
- Experiences

HOW WE WORK
Axis design is known globally as a leader in universal design. We apply a wide range of design methods to assist corporations and startups prototype and build solutions to real problems for real people.

OUR VALUES
- We are optimistic
- We collaborate with clients
- We are cross-disciplinary
- We build and test our design solutions
- We are responsible
- We are efficient

INDUSTRIES
- Manufactured goods
- Services
- Government
- Medical
- Education

LOCATIONS
- London
- Shanghai
- Los Angeles
- New York

Learn more at Axisdesign.com

ABOUT US

BACKGROUND

Phasellus nec erat nibh, id convallis orci, consectetuer adipiscing elit. Maec sed diam nonum nibh euismod tincidunt ut laoreet dolore magna aliquam erat volutpat. Ut wisi enim ad minim veniam, quis nostrud exerci tation ullamcorper suscipit lobortis nisl ut aliquip ex ea commodo consequat. Duis autem vel eum iriure dolor in hendrerit in vulputate velit esse molestie consequat. Aenean placerat sem sit amet odio. Vel illum dolore eu feugiat nulla facilisis at vero eros et accumsan.

This is another form for the company overview. Place this section near the front of your proposal if you have not worked with the client before of in the end sections if the cleint knows your organization

EXPERIENCE

Proin enim sapien, augue duis dolore eu, bibendum fermentum nunc. Mauris viverra erat a ipsum facilisis eu tristique turpis luctus. Ut consectetur condimentum justo et imperdiet. Nullam urna urna, luctus non lacinia nec, tincidunt non odio. Cum sociis natoque penatibus et magnis dis parturient montes, nascetur ridiculus mus. Lorem ipsum dolor sit amet, consectetuer adipiscing elit duis autem vel eum iriure dolor in hendrerit in vulputate velit esse molestie consequat. Aenean placerat sem sit.

PHILOSOPHY

Phasellus nec erat nibh, id convallis orci, consectetuer adipiscing elit. Maec sed diam nonummy nibh euismod tincidunt ut laoreet dolore magna aliquam erat volutpat. Ut wisi enim ad minim veniam, quis nostrud exerci tation ullamcorper suscipit lobortis nisl ut aliquip ex ea commodo consequat. Duis autem vel eum iriure dolor in hendrerit in vulputate velit esse molestie consequat. Aenean

AWARDS

IN THIS SECTION
List a short list of relevant awards that show that you are respected in your area of industry and that you have the skills to successfully complete the project

HOW LONG SHOULD THIS SECTION BE?
This section should be between one paragraph to half a page.

EXAMPLE OF
LIST OF AWARDS

2017
Industrial Designers Association Of America 1 1
3 IDEA Gold Award
2 IDEA Silver Awards
1 IDEA Bronze Awards

2016
Industrial Designers Association Of America 1 1
2 IDEA Gold Award
1 IDEA Silver Awards
1 IDEA Bronze Awards

2015
Industrial Designers Association Of America 1 1
2 IDEA Gold Award
2 IDEA Silver Awards
1 IDEA Bronze Awards

PROJECT TEAM

Promote a team strength that will help you carry out the project plan. Make sure that you are able to support your claim with evidence. Present your key value proposition through the descriptions of your project team.

IN THIS SECTION
Explain how your project team is uniquelyqualified to carry out the project.

How much information you provide about qualifications will depend on the context you are operating within.
New clients might appreciate more in-depth background information. Think about ways to turn your weaknesses into strengths. You may be a newcomer to a field, for example, but could present yourself as having a fresh and energized perspective

Your client wants to know the people who will be working on a project and their credentials. What are the experiences, educational achievements, and other credentials of the personnel? Has anyone received any special training related to the project? You may also explain relevant past achievements of the personnel. Also highlight any similar project successes the organization/company has taken on in the past. Show a range of cross disciplinary expertise in design, management and technology.

Source:adapted from ndsu.edu Generic proposal structure.

HOW LONG SHOULD THIS SECTION BE?
This section should be between half a page and three pages.

EXAMPLE OF PROJECT TEAM SECTION

TEAM OVERVIEW
Lorem ipsum dolor sit amet, consectetur adipiscing elit. Nulla ac magna sed nisl tempus volutpat. Phasellus eleifend quam eros, sed tincidunt sapien facilisis eget. Praesent sodales ornare ante,

RUSS ATKINSON

Project Manager

ELLEN BARNES

Senior Designer

Russ Atkinson, senior partner, will be your primary project contact. Russ has managed over 800 projects for international corporations and has 30 years project management experience. Russ has a doctorate in mechanical engineering and medicine from the Baroque School of Modernism.

Russes achievements include 106 national and international design awards, the 2014 Nobel Prize in literature and the 2016 Prioritizer Architecture Award.

Ellen will be the lead industrial designer working on your project. Ellen designed the Eiffel Tower, the Golden Gate Bridge and 23 De Walter super cars. Ellen has a Masters degree in Product Design from Barnum Elephant University.

Ellen's achievements include 114 national and international design awards, the 2015 Nobel Prize in literature and the 2016 Prioritizer Product Award.

EXAMPLE OF CLIENTS LIST

OUR CLIENTS INCLUDE

In this section select companies that are known to your client and relevant to the proposal.

How long should this section be? This section should be half to two pages

Air Los Angeles
Sord Motor Company
Hottech
BT&B
GSTA
Rufthansa
EKEA
Bariott
Hayho Clinic
Mony
Hamsung
Royal Academy of Shoes
Boogle
Realcase
Hoyota
Wisa
American Getpress
Mirgin Atlantic
Mike
Bicrosoft
Death Valley Oceanographic Institute

EXAMPLE OF CLIENTS LIST

Lorem ipsum dolor sit amet, consectetur adipiscing elit. Nulla ac magna sed nisl tempus volutpat. Phasellus eleifend quam eros, sed tincidunt sapien facilisis eget. Praesent sodales ornare ante, quis hendrerit dolor facilisis sed. Quisque ultricies cursus felis.

 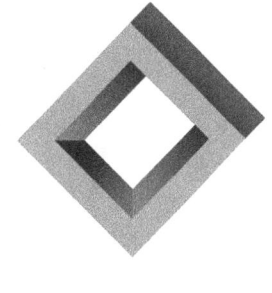

BIG RED CORP

Project: Electro Cardiograph

Lorem ipsum dolor sit amet, consectetur adipiscing elit. Integer nec odio. Praesent libero. Sed cursus ante dapibus diam. Sed nisi. Nulla quis sem at nibh elementum imperdiet. Duis sagittis ipsum. Praesent mauris. Fusce nec tellus sed augue semper porta. Mauris massa. Vestibulum lacinia arcu eget nulla.

Lorem ipsum dolor sit amet, consectetur adipiscing elit. Integer nec odio. Praesent libero. Sed cursus ante dapibus diam. Sed nisi. Nulla quis sem at nib.

WIDGET CORP

Project: Bionic ear

Lorem ipsum dolor sit amet, consectetur adipiscing elit. Integer nec odio. Praesent libero. Sed cursus ante dapibus diam. Sed nisi. Nulla quis sem at nibh elementum imperdiet. Duis sagittis ipsum. Praesent mauris. Fusce nec tellus sed augue.

Lorem ipsum dolor sit amet, consectetur adipiscing elit. Integer nec odio. Praesent libero. Sed cursus ante dapibus diam. Sed nisi. Nulla quis sem at nib.

CASE STUDIES

IN THIS SECTION
This section usually comprises of three short case studies. They should be relevant to the content of the proposal and help provide evidence and condifence that you can complete the project successfully.

The project descriptions should be witten to quantify the benefits of the design from the client perspective. Describe the challenges that you overcame, the user need, the market success in numbers. Select projects that are as recent as possible. Describe the range of services that you supplied.

Include as many of the following points as possible:

1. The Context and Challenge
2. Project background and description
3. The design problem or user need
4. Your unique insight
5. The project goals
6. Your solution

HOW LONG SHOULD THIS SECTION BE?
This section should be three case studies on one page or one case study per page on a total of three pages.

Prooduct case studey image By Virtuix - Email attachment from Virtuix CEO Jan Goetgeluk, CC BY-SA 3.0, https://commons.wikimedia.org/w/index.php?curid=26734465

EXAMPLE OF CASE STUDY

PROJECT
Proin enim sapien

CLIENT
Proin enim sapien

DATE
2017

PROJECT DESCRIPTION
Lorem ipsum dolor sit amet, consectetur adipiscing elit. Donec nec ipsum sit amet mauris mattis scelerisque. Ut faucibus lorem eget turpis pharetra tempus. Donec ultricies accumsan interdum. Donec id mollis est, ac tincidunt mauris. Etiam convallis eu massa et congue. Sed id interdum velit. Fusce id arcu ultrices, rhoncus magna id, interdum risus. Nulla tincidunt interdum mi sollicitudin faucibus.

SERVICES

▸ Product design
▸ Engineering
▸ Brand
▸ Tooling

Some design companies quote hourly rates for each additional service that they can offer as you see at the end of the second example on the facing page.

EXAMPLE OF ADDITIONAL SERVICES

GRAPHICS
- Product graphics
- Packaging graphics
- Web design
- Color consulting

PHOTOGRAPHY
- Photography And Art Direction
- Photoshop
- Web design

MAUFACTURING
- Injection molding
- Die casting
- Sheetmetal
- Complex assembly
- Testing & inspection
- Post molding operations
- Pad printing

PROTOTYPING
- Soft goods
- In-house 3d printing
- Foam models
- Low fidelity prototypes
- Form stuies
- Appearance models

LEGAL SERVICES
- Patents
- Copyrights
- Expert witness services
-

RESEARCH
- Focus groups
- Inteviews
- Observation
- Surveys

EXAMPLE OF ADDITIONAL SERVICES

ADDITIONAL SERVICES
Additional Services can be provided at your direction. Due to the variable nature of the work, I propose hourly compensation for Additional Services, which may include the following:

1. Additional Design Services, above and beyond the Scope of Work Variance Process (if req'd), including communication with the municipality, preparation of applications, attendance at Board of Adjustment hearings, etc.
2. Code Letters/ As-Built Drawings, including site inspection and inspection of existing conditions for letters to the town, redrafting of construction documents to reflect existing conditions which depart from the original construction documents
3. Bidding/Negotiations, including all site visits with all potential contractors, setting up all meetings, etc.
4. Construction Administration, including weekly meetings to observe the progress of the work, preparation of as-built drawings which differ from the permit set of drawings due to client revisions in the field, letters required by the municipal offices, etc.

FOR ADDITIONAL SERVICES, IHOURLY RATE COMPENSATION AS FOLLOWS:
Architect   150 $/hr
Associate   100 $/hr
Draftsman   75 $/hr
Clerical   45 $/hr

Source: Adapted from Joseph M. Marchese

The additional services section offers the designer the opportunity to make the client aware of additional activities that may be needs on the project that the client has not requested in the proposal. Allow a suitable margin for managing and subcontracting the work if that is your intention.

TERMS & CONDITIONS

WHAT ARE TERMS & CONDITIONS?
Terms and Conditions for the project usually form part of the design proposal and the client agrees to those conditions in writing before design work is carried out.

Terms and conditions form a legally binding contract between you and the client.
Terms and Conditions should cover all aspects of the design activity, including fees, copyright, amendments to the design and interactions with third parties. Terms and Conditions will protect your interests, clarify the expectations of each party, and prevent disputes.

You should have your terms drafted or reviewed by your attorney. These notes will help you make the best use of his or her time and expertise.

DO I NEED TERMS & CONDITIONS?
Terms clarify the terms under which a client is purchasing services from you. They help avoid any misunderstandings between you and your clients.

I SELL OVERSEAS. DO I NEED WORLDWIDE TERMS AND CONDITIONS?
It would be a mammoth task to write Terms for every legal jurisdiction in the world.
1. Include a Governing Law clause in your "T&Cs" that states where your business is located and the law under which your Terms of business are governed.
2. Start with Terms and Conditions written for your local legal juristiction and once your business grows have Terms written for your other major markets.

YOUR TERMS AND CONDITIONS ARE LEGALLY BINDING
Terms and Conditions will not stop you from being sued, they will help your case, provide evidence of your terms of business, provide protection and, may limit your liability. A compny's terms and conditions are copyright to that organization. An attorney here in California may charge three to six thousand dollars to draft a set from scratch. Some design associations such as AIGA offer standard sets to their members.
1. Make sure your terms are

easy to understand
2. Lay out your terms with clear headers.
3. Make your terms fair and reasonable.
4. Don't use small print. Doing so makes it seem like you're hiding something.
5. Use your firm's name and the client's name throughout the document instead of the generic terms "client" and "designer."
6. Eliminate legal words such as, "hereof" and "thereto."
7. Point out what is required of your client in terms of information, schedules, decision-making and approvals.

CONSEQUENCES OF NON-PAYMENT.
Reserve the right to suspend work or withhold project documents if payments are not received within a reasonable period of time from invoice date.

INTRODUCTION
Design Company agrees to provide the services (the "Services") described in this Agreement ("Agreement") to the Client identified in this Agreement (the "Client"), in accordance with the following Terms and Conditions. Please consider this Agreement good for 30 days.

RETRIEVAL FEE
Charge a fee to transfer electronic design files from archive to the client.

TAXES
State that the client is responsible for any applicable taxes.

EXPENSES
Clients do not usually reqire pre approval of expenses.In the US many designers use a automobile standard rate published each year by the Internal Revenue Service at www.irs.gov. Out-of-pocket travel expenses for projects are often passed on to the client at cost but all other expenses are marked up 20% or 25%. Your markup should cover your time in activities such as booking air travel.

Consider the following
- The fees quoted in the proposal usually do not include reimbursable expenses.
- Expenses include but are not limited to transportation, lodging, meals, travel incidentals and honoraria, project materials, blueprints, model supplies, long distance

- telephone calls, market research expenses facility rentals, videotaping, payment for participants, etc. and outside Services.
- When expenses are invoiced
- Markup on expenses cost plus X%.
- Standard fee schedule does not include travel time. Travel expenses are billed at cost plus X%. Travel time is billed at X% of standard hourly rates for X hours each day of travel.
- Fees are subject to fluctuations in the cost of outside services and changes or additions requested by the client.
- Upon written request, documentation of expenses will be provided.
- Quoted out-of-pocket expenses are estimates for budgeting purposes only.
- Client shall pay any applicable taxes, such as sales, use, value added or similar taxes, shipping handling and related charges General

INVOICES
State how often you will send invoices for ongoing work. Weekly, biweekly or monthly is most common or based on phases or milestones. The schedule of billing has a significant effect on your cash flow. Send the invoices by email and by regular mail if requested.

PAYMENT TERMS
Define when payment is due as a number of days, counting from the day that the invoice was issued. "Net 30" means that the client must return payment to you within 30 days. Many design firms request "Net 15" to support purchasing of ongoing project supplies from vendors on terms of "Net 30." Limit credit that you are willing to extend to a client. State that a project may be put on hold if required payments are not received.

Consider the following:
- Deposit details
- Payment terms
- Definition of hourly rates
- Transfer of intellectual property only after receiving all fees for the project.
- Late payment charges. Local state or national laws may apply.
- Fees for bounced cheques
- COD Payment conditions
- Right to adjust quotation if project continues over a period in excess on one year.

- Specify currency of payment.
- Cost estimates are based on understanding of scope
- Design company reserves the right to re-quote cost estimates upon completion of each stage based on new information.

LATE PAYMENT PENALTIES

Most design firms charge clients a late fee of 1.5% per month or 18% per year. Some US states have legal limits on interest charged. The interest should be aded as a line item on monthly statements. Apply client payments first to the penalty charges, and then to the unpaid balance on the oldest unpaid invoice. Make any transfer of IP rights based upon receipt of full payment from the client for your services.

CHANGES

Bill client changes on a time- and- materials basis, and give your standard hourly rate. Before commencing a change that is outside the scope of your original proposal provide the client with a change order. Describe in the change order the amount of additional time and money required only commnce the change work whn you have received the change order with authorized signature.

A change order is a mini-proposal. You'll want to reference the original proposal and state that the same terms and conditions will apply.
A change order can be based on time-and-materials or be a fixed fee. Change orders should be invoiced separately. Define a substantive change as being anything that exceeds a certain percentage of the original schedule such as 10% or a certain dollar amount and for these larger changes draft a proposal rather than a change order.
- Client agrees to renegotiate the Fees and execute a Change Order
- reserves the right to withhold Services while such Change Orders are being negotiated.

TIME

Specify that if a client causes a lengthy delay it will result in a day-for-day extension of the project's final deadline. Some firms charge a delay penalty

ACCEPTANCE

Work delivered to the client should be considered accepted unless the client notifies you to the contrary within 5 to 10 days.

ACCREDITATION
State that, once the project has been completed and introduced to the public, you will add the client's name to your client list and can enter the work into design competitions. If you have licensed the final design to the client rather than making a full assignment of rights, and the work does not fall within the category of work-for-hire you are legally entitled to show the work in your portfolio.

WORK FOR HIRE
"In the United States, a work made for hire is a work created by an employee as part of their job, or where all parties agree in writing to the WFH designation. It is an exception to the general rule that the person who actually creates a work is the legally recognized author of that work. According to copyright law in the United States and certain other copyright jurisdictions, if a work is "made for hire", the employer—not the employee—is considered the legal author. In some countries, this is known as corporate authorship. The entity serving as an employer may be a corporation or other legal entity, an organization, or an individual"
Source: Wikipedia

CONFIDENTIAL INFORMATION
Confidentiality should be included in your terms even if you've already signed a sep- arate confidentiality and non-disclosure agreement You may specify that confidentiality and non-disclosure to be mutual so that your own proprietary information is protected as well.

NO SOLICITATION
Insert a clause saying that your client may not solicit members of your design firm to join their organization.

NON EXCLUSIVITY
If a client wants to be your only client in a particular category, your pricing should be much higher in order to offset that lost business.

DISCLAIMER OF WARRANTIES
Some states require by law that the disclaimer language be sufficiently "conspicuous" Use ALL CAPS or in type that is larger or in a contrasting color, for a disclaimer of any warranty,

LIMITATIONS ON LIABILITY
Specify that your client not recover any damages from you

in excess of the total amount of money agreed to in the proposal. You cannot contract away the rights of any third party to make a claim.Some states require by law that the Limitations Of Liability language be sufficiently "conspicuous" Use ALL CAPS or in type that is larger or in a contrasting color, for a disclaimer of any warranty,

FORCE MAJEURE

French term that means "superior force." It refers to any event or effect that cannot be reasonably anticipated or controlled such as a war, a labor strike, extreme weather or an earthquake it may terminate the project without finding fault with the designer or client.

TERM AND TERMINATION

Defines the process for terminating the project, in the event of an unforseen need, from notification through calculation of your final invoice. That final billing might cover time and materials for actual services performed through the date of cancellation, or it might be a lump-sum cancellation fee, or perhaps a combination of the two. Usually the designer will retain IP.

- Specify currency of payment.
- Cost estimates are based on understanding of scope
- Design company reserves the right to re-quote cost estimates upon completion of each stage based on new information.

LATE PAYMENT PENALTIES

Most design firms charge clients a late fee of 1.5% per month or 18% per year. Some US states have legal limits on interest charged. The interest should be aded as a line item on monthly statements. Apply client payments first to the penalty charges, and then to the unpaid balance on the oldest unpaid invoice. Make any transfer of IP rights based upon receipt of full payment from the client for your services.

CHANGES

Bill client changes on a time- and- materials basis, and give your standard hourly rate. Before commencing a change that is outside the scope of your original proposal provide the client with a change order. Describe in the change order the amount of additional time and money required only commnce the change work whn you have received the change order with authorized signature.

A change order is a mini-proposal. You'll want to reference the original proposal and state that the same terms and conditions will apply.
A change order can be based on time-and-materials or be a fixed fee. Change orders should be invoiced separately. Define a substantive change as being anything that exceeds a certain percentage of the original schedule such as 10% or a certain dollar amount and for these larger changes draft a proposal rather than a change order.
- Client agrees to renegotiate the Fees and execute a Change Order
- reserves the right to withhold Services while such Change Orders are being negotiated.

TIME
Specify that if a client causes a lengthy delay it will result in a day-for-day extension of the project's final deadline. Some firms charge a delay penalty

ACCEPTANCE
Work delivered to the client should be considered accepted unless the client notifies you to the contrary within 5 to10 days.

ACCREDITATION
State that, once the project has been completed and introduced to the public, you will add the client's name to your client list and can enter the work into design competitions. If you have licensed the final design to the client rather than making a full assignment of rights, and the work does not fall within the category of work-for-hire you are legally entitled to show the work in your portfolio.

WORK FOR HIRE
"In the United States, a work made for hire is a work created by an employee as part of their job, or where all parties agree in writing to the WFH designation. Work for hire is a statutorily defined term (17 U.S.C. § 101), so a work for hire is not created merely because parties to an agreement state that the work is a work for hire. It is an exception to the general rule that the person who actually creates a work is the legally recognized author of that work. According to copyright law in the United States and certain other copyright jurisdictions, if a work is "made

Terms & conditions **159**

for hire", the employer—not the employee—is considered the legal author. In some countries, this is known as corporate authorship. The entity serving as an employer may be a corporation or other legal entity, an organization, or an individual"
*Source: Wikipedia*This is the legal jurisdiction governing the project. Identify the state whose laws will govern the signed agreement. Your client will often request the state where their office is located.

"This Agreement is governed by the laws of XX without application of its conflicts of law principles. Any claims brought under this Agreement shall be subject to jurisdiction of the state or federal courts in XX"

DISPUTE RESOLUTION
There are three standard types of dispute resolution.

MEDIATION
A non-binding intervention between parties in an informal setting in order to promote resolution of a dispute. . There are professional mediators and lawyers who offer mediation services.

ARBITRATION
an impartial third party (an arbitrator) hears both sides of the dispute in an out-of- court setting. The arbitrator is an attorney who acts much like a judge, listening to both sides of the story but not actively participating in discussion. After hearing the facts, the arbitrator will make a decision. In your contract, you will specify whether the decision of the arbitrator is binding or non-binding. The fees involved might be large

GOVERNING LAW

This is the legal jurisdiction governing the project. Identify the state whose laws will govern the signed agreement. Your client will often request the state where their office is located.

"This Agreement is governed by the laws of XX without application of its conflicts of law principles. Any claims brought under this Agreement shall be subject to jurisdiction of the state or federal courts in XX"

DISPUTE RESOLUTION

There are three standard types of dispute resolution.

MEDIATION

A non-binding intervention between parties in an informal setting in order to promote resolution of a dispute. . There are professional mediators and lawyers who offer mediation services.

ARBITRATION

an impartial third party (an arbitrator) hears both sides of the dispute in an out-of- court setting. The arbitrator is an attorney who acts much like a judge, listening to both sides of the story but not actively participating in discussion. After hearing the facts, the arbitrator will make a decision. In your contract, you will specify whether the decision of the arbitrator is binding or non-binding. The fees involved might be large (depending on the dispute, they could easily range from $3,000 to $20,000 or more), but usually they are less than those involved in pursuing a lawsuit.

LITIGATION

means that you are pursuing a lawsuit through the court system in order to resolve a dispute. The time and expense involved may be considerable

ATTORNEYS' FEES

Under copyright law, a winning plaintiff is entitled to recover his or her attorneys' fees if the copyright was regis- tered before the infringement occurred. For other types of liability, the obligation to pay the prevailing party's legal expenses must be established in your contract.

FINAL AGREEMENT.
This Agreement is the entire Agreement between the parties regarding the Services and supersedes all prior and contemporaneous greements, verbal or written. This Agreement may only be amended by a writing executed by both parties.

AUTHORIZATION TO PROCEED
Consider
- State that the ATP must be signed by authorized person in client and design company to be a legally binding contract between both organizations.
- Consequences of changes of scope.
- Work change orders.
- Client reposnisbility for paying fees
- Cancellation fees

ASSIGNMENT
Neither party may assign this Agreement or any of its rights or obligations hereunder without the prior written consent of the other party, which consent will not be unreasonably withheld.

SEVERABILITY
State consequences if If any provision of the Agreement is held illegal or unenforceable by a court of competent jurisdiction.

RELATIONSHIP OF PARTIES.
The parties are independent contractors and not permitted to create binding agreements on behalf of the other party.

NOTICES AND COMMUNICATIONS
Definet methods of communicationand when they will be effective.

FORCE MAJEURE
Define consequences of non performace by either party due to war or human or natural catastrophy.

CLIENT REVIEW
Stae that the client is responsible for final review, testing and approval

DAMAGES WAIVER
- Either party will not be liable to the other for any consequential damages.
- Specify details.
- Specify consequences of 3rd party actions

LIMITATION OF LIABILITY
- Specify maximum liability.
- Sometimes limited to design fees.

TERMINATION
- How termination should be notified
- Conditions of termination

INTELLECTUAL PROPERTY
Specify that the design company will be listed as the inventor on patents

NON-DISCLOSURE OF CONFIDENTIAL INFORMATION
- Each Party agrees not to use any Confidential Information of the other Party for any purpose other than as provided under the terms of this Agreement, and (ii) to limit disclosure of Confidential Information.
- Specify Confidentiality provisions
- Design company will require subcontractors to sign non-disclosure agreement.

PHOTOGRAPHS OF THE PROJECT
After completion of an environmental/3-D project (such as a signage system, a trade show booth, a retail interior or an exhibit) you need the right to photograph the result. This involves being able to access it and take your photographs under optimal circumstances.

CLIENT INSURANCE
Ask your client to provide you with proof that they have adequate insurance coverage in place for the duration of the project

DESIGNER INSURANCE
Large clients often specify minimum insurance levels for the designer's business. Standard business requirements include general liability, workers comp and automobile coverage. In addition, you may need to carry professional liability insurance to cover such things as intellectual property infringement or errors and omissions. If designer insurance requirements are added to the agreement, you must provide proof of coverage in the form of a certificate of insurance that is sent from your insurance agent directly to the client.

FAILURE RULE

BUSINESSES FAIL MOST OFTEN DUE TO ONE OR MORE OF THESE FOUR ISSUES:

1. INADEQUATE SALES (39%)
2. COMPETITIVE WEAKNESSES (21%)
3. EXCESSIVE OPERATING EXPENSES (11%)
4. UNCOLLECTED RECEIVABLES (9%)

Source:bplans.com

SOME INDUSTRY RECOMMENDATIONS FOR TERMS & CONDITIONS

The precise wording of design terms and conditions depend on the legal jurisdiction of the client and designer and the nature of the design work that is undertaken. There are many legal differences between states in the United States that affect the wording of terms and conditions and greater differences when working transnationally.

The publication "Business and legal forms for Industrial Designers" Published by the IDSA lists the following terms for industrial designer client agreements.

1. Date
2. Address of Client
3. Address of Designer
4. Description of project
5. Scope of work in phases
6. Services to be rendered by the Designer
7. Schedule with start and end date
8. Description of how Purchases or materials and merchandise shall be handled / Whether client or designer is responsible
9. How charges will be made
10. The Client shall be responsible for the payment of sales tax, packing, shipping, and any related charges on such purchases.
11. A list of items owned by the client prior to commencement of the project
12. How charges for expenses will be made
13. Client acknowledges that this budget is subject to change and is not a guarantee on the part of the Designer with respect to the prices contained therein.
14. Schedule of meetings
15. Force Majeure statement
16. Approvals by Client.
17. Client Responsibilities.
18. Basis of renumeration
19. Deposit
20. Payment
21. Term and termination
22. Ownership of design

23. Outside consultants
24. Publicity
25. Assignment
26. Relationship off parties
27. Arbitration
28. Legal jurisdiction
29. Designer Authorized signatory and date
30. Client Authorized signatory and date

The publication "Employing a Designer" By Peter J. Leslie, Design Council lists the following recommended terms for an industrial design contract.

1. Subject
2. Validity
3. Scope of work
4. Place of work
5. Fees and Expenses
6. Payments
7. Assignments
8. Confidentiality
9. Indemnity
10. Sub-contract
11. Termination
12. Notices
13. Exclusion of terms
14. Arbitration and law

THE CONTRACT SHOULD BE SIGNED BEFORE THE DESIGNER STARTS WORK

NEVER WORK WITHOUT A SIGNED AUTHORIZATION TO PROCEED AND A DEPOSIT BASED ON A DETAILED PROPOSAL

06
PAYMENT

RECIPE FOR A SUCCESSFUL PROJECT

1. Have a strong, human and experienced project manager
2. Communicate efficiently and frequently with all thestakeholders Manage the schedule rigorously
3. Manage scope rigorously
4. Co-manage with the client
5. Follow a tested and successful process Over deliver and under promise
6. Work with the best people
7. Keep upper management informed and engaged

BRAD EGELAND
Project manager

PAYMENT

An estimate for the number of design hours and the estimated duration of the work for each phase. The duration and the design hours are usually different because the duration depends on the number of other projects on which the designer is working and on factors such as client approval. Provide totals of estimates for the whole project.

The first phase is often quoted at a fixed price and later phases are estimated which may be revised if necessary before the commencement of each phase. In the United states a deposit is usually required for 30% or 50% of design hours prior to commencement of each phase. Clients who do not intend to pay fees will always seek to aviod paying a deposit so it is my advice not to proceed without a deposit. It is a way of identifying those cleints who intend not to pay you.

Expenses are usually quoted separately. They typically may include things like travel, accommodation, art supplies, and research costs. There is normally a 20% to 25% markup on the designer's costs when they are passed on to the client.

Include:
- Hours worked
- Duration or elapsed time of each phase
- Fees for each phase without disbursements.
- State disbursements will be added
- Later stages TBD
- Very rarely will you find a client who will pay you on time.
- Inform them at what stages during a project you want to be compensated.
- This is the area where you'll lay out the production schedule, along with how and when you get paid.
  - Allow yourself some breathing room. under-promise and over-deliver.
  - Add 10% to 20% contingency to keep yourself covered.
  - Things usually take longer than you initially expect.

CALCULATING YOUR HOURLY RATE

It is important to consider tax when calculating your hourly rate

EXPENSES
Calculate your annual business expenses.
lPrepare a worksheet with estimated amounts.

GENERAL EXPENSES
- Office rent and utilities
- If you work from a home office, these will be prorated amounts.
- Office telephone and Internet access
- Office supplies
- Computer hardware and software
- Liability insurance
- Advertising and marketing expenses
- Business travel and client entertainment
- Legal and accounting services
- Business taxes and licenses
- Depreciation
- Depreciation of furniture and fixtures

LABOR EXPENSES
Salary
Health insurance
Other employee benefits
Employer taxes

BILLABLE HOURS
Calculate your billable hours

Full-time schedule 52 wks x 40 hrs
Less: Vacation 3 wks x 40 hrs
Sick time   4 days x 8 hrs
Public holidays 10 days x 8 hrs
Marketing   50 wks x 14 hrs
Total billable hours available 1,148

Employees in smaller firms have fewer billable hours because they need to spend relatively more time on activities like marketing. A sustainable small designer firm manager pends 40 to 60% of their time on marketing activities which include writing proposals.

BREAKEVEN RATE
Divide the total expenses by the total billable hours available. This gives you a breakeven rate, meaning that you have to charge at least that much per hour in order to stay in business.

BILLING RATE
The typical profit margin for an average design business in the US is between 10 and 20 percent. Add this to your break even rate to calculate your billable rate

LOOK AT THE COMPETITION
Compare your rates to thoses of other designers in your area. Rates vary according to design discipline. Review and adjust your rates once or twice per year. Never bill below your break even point.

Source: AIGA Shel Perkins August 2006.

HOW TO FIND THE CLIENT'S BUDGET

Writing too many unsuccessful proposals will cause a small design company to struggle financially. Each proposal costs you between $300 and $3,000 in billable time. One of the most successful things that you can do to increase your profitability is to increase the successrate of proposals. Just knowing that your prospective client's budget is realistic can double your succees rate because you do not write proposals for clients who do not have the budget to hire you.

Some advice from Designer Jake Jorgovan

"There are two simple ways that I recommend figuring out the client's budget.

When the client first inquires about the project, I always ask a series of questions.

1. One of the questions I always ask is, "Do you have a budget set aside for this project and is it over X?" This first weeds out low budget clients, and often clients will respond and let you know the budget that they have available. Just asking for the budget goes a long way. The client won't always reveal this but if you don't ask you will never know.

2. The ballpark question - Often clients will ask you for a ballpark quote for the project. Whenever I get this question I answer with a wide spectrum. I say something like, "It could cost anywhere from $1,000-$8,000 depending on the scope. Did you have a budget in mind that you were looking to spend?"

SOLO DESIGNERS HOURLY RATES

Source Data for Graphic Design How Magazine 2014 996 responses Core77 and industry associations do international annual reviews of industry rates.

	Average	Low	High
Northeast	$74	$37.50	$150
Midwest	$65	$25	$110
West	$67	$20	$150
South	$68	$25	$350

WHERE DO YOU WORK?
46% Solo design practice or full-time freelance business
17% Graphic design firm
31% In-house design department

WHAT KIND OF HOURLY RATE DO YOU USE?
61% Blended (a single, averaged rate for all billable functions)
32% Different rates per task (such as proofreading, design, strategy)
2% Different rates per seniority level (creative directors charge more than junior designers)
6% Other

HOW DID YOU DETERMINE YOUR HOURLY RATE?
28% Based on a formula including overhead, salaries and other financial factors
46% Based on common rates for design in my area
37% Based on a best guess or gut feeling
13% Other

DO YOU SHARE YOUR HOURLY RATE WITH CLIENTS?
82% Yes
18% No

DO YOU USE A TIME-TRACKING SYSTEM?
44% Yes
56% No

DO YOU HAVE A "PAIN IN THE A@@" UP-CHARGE?
40% Yes
60% No

DO YOU HAVE A RUSH FEE?
40% Yes
60% No

PRICING MODELS

When design firms sell work, there are several very different ways to structure the compensation. The most common formats are:

1. Time and materials
2. Retainer
3. Fixed-fee
4. Use-based pricing
5. Royalties
6. Hybrid
7. Free

TIME AND MATERIALS
You track the hours spent on design work using time sheets and bill the client at agreed-upon hourly rates. In addition, you track out-of-pocket expenses and bill the client sperately for reimbursement.

Travel expenses are usually reimbursed at cost, but all other expenses should be subject to a standard markup of 20% or 25% percent. The markup covers the time you spend making those purchases. Designers provide the client with a bill breaking down hours worked and expenses usually each month, or every two weeks or at the end of each stage.

FIXED-FEE
You agree with your client on a flat amount that will be charged for design services. With this type of billing how much profit you make depends on how well you manage your project. You must be very specific about the scope of work and what is included and what is not included. Clients usually make additional requests for work after the project has

started. When a client requests additional work send a change order document to the client that must be approved and invoiced separately. Many change orders are not approved and so you do not do the additional work.

USE-BASED
This method is used by photographers, copywriters and illustrators. The price is based on the ways in which the finished work will be used or reproduced. Talk with your client about the usage rights that they need, then sign an agreement that specifies:

1. The type of media
2. The total number of items for example, the size of the print run
3. The geographic area of distribution
4. The time period of use for example, six months

If the client later needs additional rights they must negotiate additional payments.

ROYALTIES
This is a common method used by industrial designers for manufactured items. The designer is called the licensor. The product company is the licensee. They manufacture, market, stock, distribute the product and provide customer service.

The designer is paid a percentage of the money received from net sales of the product (gross sales adjusted for any returns or discounts). This is called a royalty. Standard royalty rates vary by product category ranging from 3% to 15%. Well known designers can negotiate higher royalty rates. Some agreements guarantee a minimum amount that will be paid regardless of items sold. A portion of the royalty may be paid up front as a non-refundable advance.

HYBRID
On a large project, a hybrid approach to compensation sometimes makes the most sense. It's not unusual to see several different types of compensation included in one deal. For example, an industrial design firm might be paid a fixed fee for the initial phases of a project, followed by a royalty to be paid after the new product goes into mass production.

PRO BONO
Spec work is when a client asks you to generate a few sample ideas without hiring you. The danger is with this approach that there are companies that will approach one dozen different designers, get 50 free concepts and never hire a designer. I have experienced this type of client. This practice is common in some areas of the world. Most design associations advise their member not to do tis type of speculative work.

A "bake-off" is where the client approaches several firms and offers each of them a sum of money to produce a number of ideas. If the sum paid is reasonable for the work this type of project can lead to more creative work based on the individual designer's will to compete and win the larger long term project. Some of the finest architecture in the world such as the Bilboa Guggenheim project by Frank Gehry was initiated in a competitive bake-off.

Pro bono publico is a Latin phrase that means "for the public good." It refers to services that are donated to political, social, or religious organizations. Some design firms donate an ongoing percentage of their work, for example 3% for Pro Bono Projects.

Write a proposal for Pro Bona projects and be specific about time and materials. It is common for Pro Bono cllients to request many changes and meetings.

Source: Shel Perkins

ROYALTY AGREEMENTS

WHAT IS LICENSING?
Licensing means that the designer retains the intellectual property rights to a design, and license, or "rent", the design to someone for either a one-time use, such as in a magazine or advertising campaign, or for a longer term use to manufacture.

The most common methods of design licensing are:
1. Royalty: this is where the manufacturer pays the artist a royalty percentage of their gross sales.
2. Royalty with advance at the start .which is later deducted from future royalties.
3. Flat fee – a one-time fee is paid instead of royalties

The parties to a contract are free to agree the terms they choose, depending on their objectives. It is necessary to have royalty agreements in writing. They can be defined in scope by, time and territory.

Many royalty agreements do not make it to market so designers are wise to negotiate agreements with several companies to reduce risk.

WORKING WITH AN ATTORNEY
Prepare and review the contract in carefully, Get advice from an IP lattorney who works regularly with designers in your field. Informformation here does not constitute legal advice. the author is not an attorney. Laws are different in different legal juristictions. Deals that exceed the value of the attorney

Methods of Payment   179

fees need a long form contract and you need to work with an attorney

ROYALTY PERCENTAGES
Royalty payments are calculated based on the total (gross) revenues generated by the manufacturer for your products.
1. The pecentage varies according to The type of product being produced
2. The quantities expected to be sold
3. The reputation of the artist or brand

SALES VOLUME
The expected sales helps determine royalty rates. Usually the higher the volume, the lower the royalty. Larger retailers demand lower prices, which means lower profit margins for the manufacturer. Sales volume is influenced by competition, the product price and the geographical coverage of the patents.

If the products will be sold in low volume stores and in smaller quantities, the royalty rate is usually higher.

FLAT FEE PAYMENT
A flat fee is paid up front at the time the contract is signed. Royalties are not paid later. This approach is best when your cient is a small company that has low volume sales, or is a start-up company that does not have distribution. If the product sells above expectations, you may earn less than you would with ongonig royalties. You can limit the term, to one year or eighteen month contractand when they renegotiate the next term you can negotiate for a better deal.

The amount that you are able to negotiate will depend upon:
1. Your reputation
2. the competition
3. What the licensee is willing to pay

With a flat fee payment ou will be paid even if the licensee does not sell a single product. This is not uncommon.

ADVANCES
Sometimes royalties include an advance payment. For example the licensee may pay a lumpsum royalty of $50,000 on execution of agreement together with royalty of 4% of the 'net sales value' for all licensed products for a period of 6 years, commencing 2 years from the date of starting production.

If you need to conribute significant time for the agreement up front then you should ask for an advance to reduce your risk because many royalty agreements do not result in significant royalties to the designer.

This approach gives you the security of covering your costs, with the potential for higher returns if your design is commercially successful.

The designer is paid at the time of signing the contract. The advance is usually non-refundable, and is deducted from future royalty payments. Once the contract is signd, the royalties often do not start for one or two years. The advance shows commitment and helps identify the serious clients.

ROYALTIES ONLY:
This is best with larger companies with established districution channels and the risk of low sales is less. If the licesee is inexperienced then the risk of not getting the product to market is high. More than 75% of new products introduced to the market each year are not successful. The risk of failure is higher in new geographical markets.

MINIMUM ROYALTIES
There may be minimum and maximum (cut-off) royalty amounts specified in the contract. Minimum royalties motivate the licensee to put the resources behind the product to bring it to market. A maximum royalty can be negotiated when the licensor agrees that the amount will satisfy their objectives. An alternative is a reducing royalty if large volumes are expected in the future.

Designer should be guaranteed a minimum royalty payment of XX Thousand US Dollars (US $XX,000) for each of the first X years after execution of this agreement which shall be paid by the Company regardless of sales of products bearing the Designs.
The Company shall use its best efforts to promote production, marketing, distribution and sales of its products bearing the Designs. If the Company one (1) year after the commencement of production should sell less than the equivalent of a royalty amount of XX Thousand US Dollars (US $XX,000) per financial year, the Designer shall be entitled

to cancel this Agreement.

EXCLUSIVE
You promise the licensee that you will not grant any other licences to third parties or exploit the IP yourself.

SOLE
A sole licence is an agreement where you promise not to grant the same
license to any third party but you retain the right to exploit the IP yourself.

NON-EXCLUSIVE
A non-exclusive licence gives someone else the right to use your work but you retain the right to grant further licences.

WHAT IS THE BEST ROYALTY RATE?
The best royalty rate is the maximum royalty rate that the licensee is willing to pay that meets the minimum royalty rate the designer is willing to accept. Published lists based on current deals often show a wide range of percentages for a particular industry. It is helpful to know what that range is but it will not tell you precisely what is correct for your your product.
If the manufacturing business you are dealing with is inexperienced there is a high possibility that you will not earn any royalty.

25% RULE.
"It's often accepted (as a rule of thumb) that a royalty rate equalling about one-quarter of the licensee's anticipated pre-tax profits derived from the technology is a fair rate.

Of course, one needs to then determine net profits. Thus, the rates depend on the market forces of each particular product. For example, if the licensee will have profit margins of 80%, the royalty paid to the licensor should be about 20% of pre-tax, net revenues. Conversely, if profits of 4% are expected, the royalty should be within the range of 1-1.5% of net revenues earned." *Source: Stephen Jenei*

Therefore, the 25% Rule is a starting point
One needs to consider:
1. Is the technology a breakthrough innovation?
2. Is the intellectual property strong?
3. Is the design unique?
4. Will the design require substantial R&D or regulatory clearance to bring to market?
5. What is the risk of failure?
6. What is the profit margin?

RIGHT TO AUDIT
The section of the contract that describes the designer's right to audit the licensee's books is particularly important. There are many ways that a licessee ca avoid paying the designer royalties for sales. This section should be prepared for you by a qualified and experienced design IP attorney who is knowledgeable about the legal juristictions that your agreement covers.
Some things to consider:
1. The licessee should establish and maintain a reasonable accounting system that enables designer to readily identify the licessee's assets, expenses, costs of goods, and use of funds.

2. The designer and its authorized representatives shall have the right to audit, to examine, and to make copies of all financial and related records (in whatever form they may be kept, including, but not limited to those kept by thelicessee, its employees, agents, assigns, successors, and subcontractors.
3. Define a complete and extensive list of types of documents that can be examined and audited.
4. Define the term for maintaining records such as during the term of the agreement and for a period of ten years after the completion of the agreement subject to a three day written notice or without prior notice.
5. Licessee should ensure the designer has these rights with licessee's employees, agents, assigns, successors, and subcontractors, and the obligations of these rights shall be explicitly included in any subcontracts or agreements formed between the licessee and any subcontractors
6. Costs of any audits conducted under the authority of this right to audit should be borne by licensee. I
7. If the audit identifies overcharges of any nature by the licensee to the designer in excess of 0.5% of the total contract billings, the licensee shall reimburse designer for the total costs of the audit.
8. If the audit discovers substantive findings related to fraud, misrepresentation, or nonperformance, designer will recoup the costs of the audit work from the licensee.

Methods of Payment 185

9. Any adjustments and/or payments that must be made as a result of any such audit or inspection of the licensee's invoices and/or records shall be made within 90 days from presentation of designer's findings to licensee.
10. Besides the royalty stipulated in the contract the licensee undertakes to pay to the executor an extra fee as compensation from sale of the product as compensation.
11. If the statement or payment does not occur at least (example 7) calendar days after demand by a registered letter, the Designer shall be entitled to cancel this Agreement without notice by a registered letter to the Company.
12. In case of delayed payment, interest shall be paid from the due date at a rate of (example 1.5%).

MORE INFORMATION
1. Association of University Technology Managers (AUTM)
2. Licensing Executives Society (LES) The IPO (Intellectual Property Organisation) has published a free Licensing Guide to learn more about how to license your intellectual property.
3. ACID is a membership organisation to help protect your intellectual property, who also might be able to help you as they sell standardised licensing agreements.
4. Design and Artists Copyright Society (DACS)

EXAMPLE OF CALCULATION OF THE EXTRA FEE IN CASE OF INFRINGEMENT OF CONDITIONS OF THE PAYMENTS

DATE	0.09.2018	0.09.201	1.12.2018	31.03.2019
The first payment	+0,003 USD	+0,006 USD	+0,012 USD	+0,024 USD
The second payment		+0,003 USD	+0,006 USD	+0,012 USD
The third payment			+0,012 USD	+0,006 USD
The fourth payment				+0,003 USD

There should be a significant deterant to cheating on royalty payments. This is an example of an escalating penalty which may help you get paid for all sales. The extra fee as compensation is paid by the licensee to the to the designer in current 3 years.

SOME HISTORICAL AVERAGE ROYALTY RATES

CATEGORY	SURVEYS	AVERAGE ROYALTY
Accessories	1	8.9%
Aerospace	3	4.0%
Apparel	3	6.8%
Automotive	8	3.3%
Baby Goods	1	6.0%
Baked Goods	1	5.2%
Books – Softcover	1	7.5%
Books – Hardcover	1	10.0%
Building & Construction	1	5.6%
Business Services	1	11.9%
Chemicals	7	4.3%
Child related	1	6.3%
Computers	6	4.6%
Consumer Goods	3	4.8%
Domestics	1	7.3%
Education Related	1	8.3%
Electronics	9	5.1%
Energy & Environment	4	8.0%
Entertainment	1	15.5%
Diagnostics	1	3.5%
Distribution	1	5.2%
Fast Food	1	5.1%
Food	7	4.4%
Footwear	1	10.0%
Franchises	1	5.0%
Furniture / Home Furnishes	1	7.0%
Government / University	2	7.1%
Healthcare Products / Equipment	7	6.4%
Hospitality / Leisure	2	4.5%
Housewares	1	7.0%

CATEGORY	SURVEYS	AVERAGE ROYALTY
Industrial Products	1	6.4%
Internet	2	8.2%
General Manufacturing	2	6.4%
Machine/Tools	5	4.8%
Maintenance Services	1	6.9%
Media & Entertainment	2	6.5%
Music / Video	1	7.0%
Medical Equipment	1	4.0%
Novelties / Gifts	1	8.3%
Animal Health Products	1	4.5%
Plant/Agriculture Products	1	4.0%
Printing	1	5.4%
Publishing	1	10.6%
Biotechnology	1	7.0%
Pharma & Biotech	3	5.0%
Retail	1	6.1%
Services	2	5.9%
Software	6	9.6%
Sporting Goods	2	7.7%
Telecom / Communications	3	5.8%
Toys & Games	3	9.7%
Trademarks and Copyright	1	10.6%
Greeting Cards & Giftwrap	1	3.5%
Household Items (cups, sheets, towels)	1	5.5%
Fabrics & Apparel	1	6.0%
Posters & Prints	1	10.0%
Toys & Dolls	1	5.5%

Royalty rates vary according to what is common in an industry sector, by what you are able to negotiate, by the quality of the design that you are providing, by how the design complements the other products and services being provided by the company licensing the design, and by your value and reputation. A well known designer's name associated with a product can be a type of branding. Negotiate what you can but be aware of what is realistic

ROYALTY RATES

Royalty rates vary widely. Note that royalties may be spread over a range from 0% to three times the "average royalty" and that the above average royalty rates should only be used to support royalty rates determined using first principles.

15% TO 20% FOR BEATLES PRODUCTS
Royalty rate for Beatles' products. "Beatles' products 'have the highest royalty rate, but they sell well,' Apple demands somewhere in the neighborhood of 15 percent to 20 percent in royalties on licensed products.'" The Beatles. Music royalty rates. (Peter Miniaci, owner of The Beatlemania Shoppe in Toronto quoted in Dan Higgins, "Beatles fans obtain rare license to offer product," Albany Times Union, Albany, NY, April 13, 2005)

15% OR MORE FOR COMPUTING INVENTIONS
Software licensing royalty rate paid by Dell Computers for highly marketable products. "Francine Segars, strategic commodity manager who negotiates software licensing agreements for Dell Computers [800-289-3355] in Austin, Texas, asserts that it's not unusual for an inventor to receive 15% or more in royalties for a highly marketable product." Software license royalty rates. License agreement royalty rates. (Williams-Harold, Bevolyn, "You've got it made! (developing invention ideas)," Black Enterprise, June 1, 1999)

UP TO 15%. FOR VIDEO GAME INVENTIONS
Licensing royalty rates paid for video game inventions. "The industry average for licensing is about 3 percent, but if the product has a patent, the inventor can ask for a higher royalty, [Bob DeMatteis, author of From Patent to Profit] said. It also varies

by market potential. For example, he said, the rate for a plastic flip top might be a fraction of a percentage point, but a video game could be up to 15 percent." Fliptop. Video game inventions. Video game successes. (Bob DeMatteis quoted in Thuy-Doan Le, "Entrepreneurial spirit starts to pay off for Sacramento, Calif.-area inventor," The Sacramento Bee, December 12, 2004) View the latest in newly released video game products.

In China the name of the designer or a celebrity endorsement of a product can be as valuable to consumer as the manufacturer's brand.

UP TO 10% OF WHOLESALE SALES FOR TOY INVENTIONS
"Although royalty arrangements vary greatly, the most a toy inventor can realistically expect by the time negotiations are complete is 10% (5% is more typical) of wholesale sales." Toy royalty rate. Royalty on a toy invention. What percentage does an inventor make? (Caryne Brown, "Making money making toys: how black inventors are bringing innovative ideas to the toy market", Black Enterprise, November 1, 1993)

10% FOR EDUCATIONAL GAME
"[Donna Williamson, inventor of Kinderdoos, a colorful educational game that helps children get ready for school and bedtime while teaching them independence] has a licensing agreement with Pockets of Learning, a Rhode Island-based toy distributor that specializes in heirloom-quality toys and games, that will expire in January [2008]. Until then, Pockets of Learning will manufacture, market and sell the game for Williamson, who will get

THE 25% RULE

Many royalty agreements use the relief from royalty methodology and "the 25% rule" for calculating the royalty.

According to "the 25% rule", the royalty rate is generally expected to fall within the range 25% to 33% of profits before interest and tax (PBIT). However, this "rule" only applies where:

1. The IP Is A Driver Of Sales/Profits;
2. The IP Represents A Relatively Strong Arsenal Of Assets;
3. The IP Grants The User Protection From Competition; And
4. The IP Appears To Be Valid And Enforceable

10 percent of all royalties. The suggested retail price of Kinderdoos is $24.95." Product license. (David Benda, "Necessity spurred Redding woman to create educational game," Redding Record Searchlight," Monday, November 26, 2007)

8% TO 12% OF SALES FOR WELL-KNOWN BRANDS

"Attorneys who deal with licensing issues said most companies that license well-known brands pay a royalty rate of 8 percent to 12 percent of sales. That would put TRG's [TRG Accessories] nine-month sales of the Swiss Army brand luggageSwiss Army brand luggage at $8.1 million to $12.1 million." Royalty percentage paid. (Margie Manning, "Brothers market 'James Bond' of luggage," St. Louis Business Journal, February 23, 2001)

7% LICENSING ROYALTY RATE FOR DONNA KARAN INTERNATIONAL JEANS WEAR

"[In] September 1996, Donna Karan International granted Designer Holdings Ltd. a thirty-year license to produce, sell and distribute DKNY men's and women's jeanswear. In return Donna Karan International received $60 million plus an annual 7 percent royalty on total sales and an additional 2 percent on international sales." Royalty rate statistics. (Glenn DeSouza, "Royalty methods for intellectual property," Business Economics, April 1, 1997)

5.7% LICENSING ROYALTY RATE FOR THE BLACKBERRY

In May 2003, the U.S. District Court for the Eastern District of Virginia ruled that the royalties paid by Blackberry maker, Research In Motion to Chicago inventor Thomas Campana, Jr., through his holding company, NTP, be increased to 8.55 percent, up from the 5.7 percent rate. This ruling was issued in November 2002, when a jury ruled that Research In Motion had "willfully infringed on NTP patents on wireless communications in e-mail systems." (Stuart Weinberg, "BlackBerry maker's stock falls after patent case ruling Company must pay more damages, higher royalties to inventor," Chicago Sun-Times, May 28, 2003)

5% TO 10% STANDARD PATENT ROYALTY RATES FOR TOY INVENTIONS

"[I]ndependent inventors represent a rich, yet relatively inexpensive, creative resource. By dealing with established independent inventors, toy companies can cull promising ideas from around the world, while paying only royalties of 5-10 percent for their use and development." Royalty payouts for inventions. Standard royalty rate paid to toy inventors. (Milt Schulman, "Toy inventors assume greater role," Playthings, November 1, 1992)

5% OF THE PRODUCT MANUFACTURING COST

"'The average royalty is 5 percent of the manufacturing cost of the product.' The manufacturer should give the inventor an upfront fee to show it is working in good faith. That may be anywhere from $5,000 to $150,000. 'The highest one I had was $3.1 million,' ...That's part of the negotiation. Have them make you an offer, which puts you in a counter-offering position.'" Average invention royalty rate. Royalties paid inventors. Patent licensing statistics. (Pamela H. Riddle, chief executive of Innovative Product Technologies quoted in Marcia Heroux Pounds, "Licensing Offer Inventors A Safe Path to Production," Knight Ridder/Tribune Business News, November 10, 1998)

5% OF SALES AVERAGE FOR INVENTIONS
Licensing royalty share Inventors' Publishing and Research allocates to inventors. "[Elaine] Montoya [San Francisco-based Inventors' Publishing and Research (IP&R)], like all the company's inventor-clients, gets 5% of sales for royalties, and absolutelyNEW gets 1%." What is the average royalty paid to inventors? Standard patent licensing deal percentage. (Jeffrey Gangemi, "Prototyping Gives Inventions a Boost," Business Week, November 13, 2006).

3% INDUSTRY AVERAGE LICENSING ROYALTY RATE FOR INVENTIONS
"The industry average for licensing is about 3 percent, but if the product has a patent, the inventor can ask for a higher royalty, [Bob DeMatteisBob DeMatteis, author of From Patent to Profit] said. It also varies

by market potential. For example, he said, the rate for a plastic flip top might be a fraction of a percentage point, but a video game could be up to 15 percent." Video game product licensing deals. Royalty rates percentage. What royalty rate should I expect to receive for my patent? Common royalty rate percentages. (Thuy-Doan Le, "Entrepreneurial spirit starts to pay off for Sacramento, Calif.-area inventor," The Sacramento Bee, December 12, 2004)

1% TO 4% OF SALES FOR INVENTIONS
"Many companies routinely license patents from individual inventors in exchange for a share of the revenue these products generate. Royalties usually will range between 1 and 4 percent of sales. While that may not sound like much, when you consider the resources a large company can put behind a product launch -- manufacturing, marketing, distribution -- it's not a bad deal." (E. Patrick Ellisen, "Disputes over IP rights can prove costly for all involved," Silicon Valley / San Jose Business Journal, September 3, 2004)

28.3% OF ROYALTY PAYMENTS AWARDED TO STANFORD UNIVERSITY INVENTORS
"At Stanford [University] the Office of Technology Licensing takes 15 percent off the top, and remaining royalties are split into equal thirds between the inventor, the university and the inventor's department." (Chris Rauber, "Dr. Strange Glove," San Francisco Business Times, December 5, 1997)

25% TO 33% OF NET PROFITS TO INVESTOR BACKERS
"[Y]ou might want to give some thought to getting a backer. Not a partner, a backer. In exchange for funding the legal and miscellaneous costs, the backer receives a portion of the net profits. The angel is not a partner — it's your invention, and you call the shots. The percentage for the backer [of an invention] is negotiable. If I were doing it, I'd offer my backer 25 percent, and I'd be willing to go up to a third. That's purely subjective, and your input is as valid as mine. The backer would be investing in you the same way an angel invests in a Broadway show." (Harvey Reese, How to License Your Million Dollar Idea, Second Edition, John Wiley & Sons, Inc., New York, 2002, p. 77)

10 TO 20% OF SALES TO UNIVERSITY SPONSOR
"Under a licensing agreement with the school, Environmental Robotics gives 10 to 20 percent of its sales to UNM [University of New Mexico]. " (Mohsen Shahinpoor cited in Dennis Domrazalski, NMBW Staff "Albuquerque inventor revolutionizes the field of robotics," New Mexico Business Weekly, May 28, 2004)

RETAINER AGREEMENTS

WHAT IS A RETAINER AGREEMENT?

A retainer agreement is anagreement between a designer and a client where the client gaurantees the designer a certain number of hours work each month. They are often written for a one year term which may be renewed.

WHY USE A RETAINER AGREEMENT?

They offer benefits for both the designer and their client. For the designer they provide a consistent cashflow. For the client they are able to guarantee that the designer will be available when needed and this type of agreement may be less expensive that setting up an internal design department. The designer often provide a discount on their usual hourly rate.

EXAMPLES OF RETAINER AGREEMENTS

EXAMPLE ONE

This Agreement is made between

....Designer

....Client

Services
The designer will provide the following services as of the effective date of this agreement to the client

....

....

On the signing of this Agreement, the Client shall pay a nonrefundable design fee of

$..

Thereafter, the Client shall pay a monthly retainer on the first day of each month in the amount of

$..until ....

The Designer shall render billings on a ....basis, applying the design fee and retainer payments thereto, and the Client shall pay any balance due on the billings within ....days of receipt.

The Designer's compensation shall be a design fee of $....................

Which shall start with a nonrefundable payment of $....................

by the Client, with the balance paid in installments of $....................
according to the following schedule:

If the Project continues beyond ...., an additional fee of

$....................shall be paid each month until completion.

Authorized Client signature..**Date**....................

Designer signature..**Date**....................

Methods of Payment   197

EXAMPLE TWO

This Agreement is made between

....Designer

....Client

Services
The designer will provide the following services as of the effective date of this agreement to the client

....

....

Rates
Non retainer standard rates are as follows

.... per hour

Discounts provided for retainer Agreement

Retainer Agreement Hours per month	Discount on standard rate
Less than 5 hours	7% discount
5 to 9 hours	11% discount
10 to 19 hours	15% discount
20 to 29 hours	20% discount
30 to 39 hours	25% discount
Over 40 hours	30% discount

Payment
On the effective date of this agreement the client will pay an initial retainer fee per hour for .... hours of work per month ffor the pro rated period of....................
Client understands that the rate of .... is a discounted rate.

Authorized Client signature...Date....................

Designer signature...Date....................

EXPENSES

Here is an example of the type of clause that is used for marking up expenses.

The Client agrees to reimburse the Designer for all expenses connected to the project, including but not limited to messengers, long-distance telephone calls, overnight deliveries, and local travel expenses. These expenses shall be marked up ____ percent by the Designer when billed to the Client. In the event that travel beyond the local area is required, the expenses for this travel shall be billed as follows

FLAT FEE PERCENTAGE OF COSTS

Here is an example of a flat fee clause.

Flat fee plus a percentage of costs. The Designer's compensation shall be a nonrefundable design fee of $_____ paid by the Client on the signing of this Agreement, plus an additional markup of ____ percent of the expenditures for merchandise and materials and ____ percent of the expenditures for production, except that the following budget items shall not be included in this calculation:

In the event that the Client requests design services beyond the scope of work for this Project and the Designer is able to accommodate the Client's request, the Designer shall bill for such additional services as follows.

DESIGN TODAY IS NO LONGER ABOUT DESIGNING OBJECTS, VISUALS OR SPACES; IT IS ABOUT DESIGNING SYSTEMS, STRATEGIES AND EXPERIENCES

GJOKO MURATOVSKI
Professor in design and innovation
Tongji University, Shanghai

07
USEFUL TOOLS

FIVE WHYS

WHAT IS IT
Five Whys is an iterative question method used to discover the underlying cause of a problem. For every effect there is a root cause. The primary goal of the technique is to determine the underlying cause of a problem by repeating the question "Why?"

WHO INVENTED IT
The technique was originally developed by Sachichi Toyoda Sakichi Toyoda was a Japanese inventor and industrialist. He was born in Kosai, Shizuoka. The son of a poor carpenter, Toyoda is referred to as the "King of Japanese Inventors". He was the founder of the Toyota Motor company. The method is still an important part of Toyota training, culture and success.

Sakichi Toyoda - Wikipedia, the free encyclopedia, https://en.wikipedia.org/wiki/Sakichi_Toyoda (accessed July 06, 2016).

WHY USE THIS METHOD
When we fix the root cause the problem does not reoccur

HOW TO USE THIS METHOD
1. Five whys could be taken further to a sixth, seventh, or higher level, but five is generally sufficient to get to a root cause.
2. Gather a team and develop the problem statement in agreement
3. Establish the time and place that the problem is occurring
4. Ask the first "why" of the team: why is this problem taking place?
5. Ask four more successive "whys," repeating the process
6. You will have identified the root cause when asking "why" yields no further useful information.
7. Discuss the last answers and settle on the most likely systemic cause.
8. Fix the root problem

I KEEP SIX HONEST SERVING MEN. THEY TAUGHT ME ALL I KNEW. THEIR NAMES ARE WHAT AND WHY AND WHEN AND HOW AND WHERE AND WHO

RUDYARD KIPLING
English short-story writer, poet, and novelist

WWWWWH

WHAT IS IT?
'Who, What, Where, When, Why, and How'? is a method for getting a thorough understanding of the problem, It is used to obtain basic information in police investigations. A well-known golden rule of journalism is that if you want to know the full story about something you have to answer all the five W's. Journalists argue your story isn't complete until you answer all six questions.
1. Who is involved?
2. What occurred?
3. When did it happen?
4. Where did it happen?
5. Why did it occur?

WHO INVENTED IT?
Hermagoras of Temnos, Greece 1st century BC.

WHY USE THIS METHOD?
This method helps create a story that communicates clearly the nature of an activity or event to stakeholders.

HOW TO USE THIS METHOD
1. Ask the questions starting with the 5 w's and 1 h question words.
2. Identify the people involved
3. Identify the activities and make a list of them.
4. Identify all the places and make a list of them.
5. Identify all the time factors and make a list of them.
6. Identify causes for events of actions and make a list of them.
7. Identify the way events took place and make a list of them.
8. Study the relationships between the information.

RESOURCES
Computer
Notebook
Pens
Video camera
Digital camera
Digital voice recorder
Release forms
Interview plan or structure
Questions, tasks and discussion items

SOME WWWWWH QUESTIONS

WHO
1. Is affected?
2. Who believes that the problem affects them?
3. Needs the problem solved?
4. Does not want the problem to be solved?
5. Could stand in the way of a solution?

WHEN
1. Does it happen
2. Doesn't it happen?
3. Did it start?
4. Will it end?
5. Is the solution needed?
6. Might it happen in the future?
7. Will it be a bigger problem?
8. Will it improve?

WHERE
1. Does it happen?
2. Doesn't it happen
3. Else does it happen?
4. Is the best place to solve the problem

WHY
1. Is this situation a problem?
2. Do you want to solve it?
3. Do you not want to solve it?
4. Does it not go away?
5. Would someone else want to solve it?
6. Can it be solved?
7. Is it difficult to solve?

WHAT
1. May be different in the future
2. Are its weaknesses?
3. Do you like?
4. Makes you unhappy about it?
5. Is flexible?
6. Is not flexible?
7. Do you know?
8. Do you not understand?
9. How have you solved similar problems?
10. Are the underlying ideas?
11. Are the values involved?
12. Are the elements of the problem and how are they related?
13. What can you assume to be correct
14. Is most important
15. Is least important
16. Are your goals?
17. Do you need to discover?

BENEFITS MAP

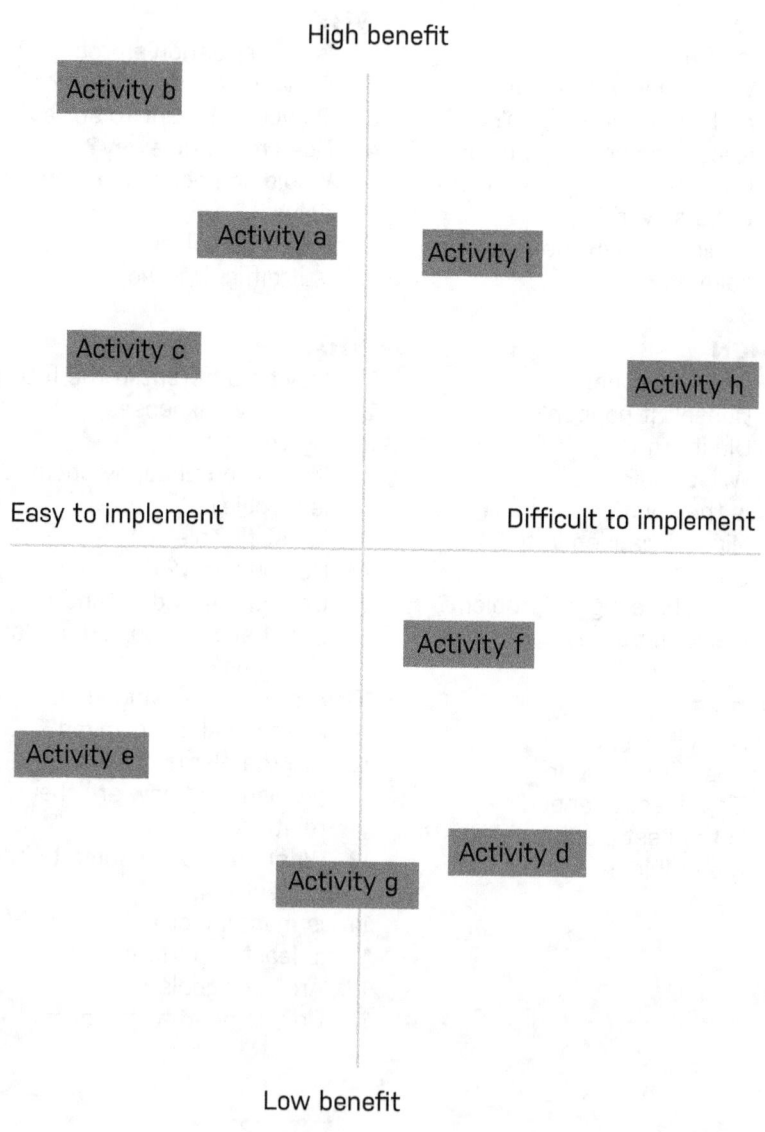

BENEFITS MAP

WHAT IS IT?
The benefits map is a simple tool that helps your team decide what will give you the best return on investment for time invested

WHY USE THIS METHOD?
1. Aids communication and discussion within the organization.
2. It is human nature to do tasks which are not most urgent first.
3. To gain competitive advantage,
4. Helps build competitive strategy
5. Helps build communication strategy
6. Helps manage time effectively

CHALLENGES
1. Can be subjective

HOW TO USE THIS METHOD
1. Moderator draws axes on Whiteboard or flip chart.
2. Worthwhile activity at the start of a project.
3. Map individual tasks.
4. Interpret the map.
5. Create strategy.
6. Tasks which have high benefit with low investment may be given priority.

RESOURCES
Pen
Paper
Whiteboard
Dry erase markers

SEGMENTATION

WHAT IS MARKET SEGMENTATION?
Market segmentation involves subdividing a market into a number of groups where the people in each group have some commonality, or similarity. Members of a market segment share something in common. Segmentation is done to provide deign solutions that work for a group of people without the expense of developing a different solution for each person. There are many ways to segment a market. The best way to segment customers depends on your goals. For example if you are entering a new global market one way is to segment your customers by where they live.

GEOGRAPHIC SEGMENTATION
This is one of the more common methods of market segmentation. For example, a company selling products in Europe may segment their customers by the country that they live in. In Europe regional differences in customer preferences exist. You may decide to segment you customers by those who live in a city and those who live in a rural location.

DISTRIBUTION SEGMENTATION
Experience maps and Service blueprints help designers understand a market where most people access multiple channels when purchasing or using a product or service

PRICE SEGMENTATION
Another common way of segmenting a market is by income. Different price-points for a product or service may appeal to people with different incomes. Mass market car companies like ford have models that appeal to people with lower incomes and luxury models that appeal to customers with higher incomes.

DEMOGRAPHIC SEGMENTATION
Demographic segmentation is possibly the most commonly used type of segmentation. There are large number of demographic factors such as gender, age, type of employment and education that are often used for segmentation. Some products and brands are targeted mainly at men. Most people over the age of 40 require glasses to read.

TIME SEGMENTATION
Some products are sold at a particular time of day or year. For example surfboards are sold in summer.

PSYCHOGRAPHIC OR LIFESTYLE SEGMENTATION
Psychographic or lifestyle segmentation, is based on, values, behaviors, emotions, perceptions, beliefs, and interests. For example some customers prefer luxury products. Some customers may follow a particular sporting team.

Markets segments should be large enough to justify creating targeted products and services. Four to six market segments is often a manageable number. Targeting too many segments is sometimes unsuccessful. Products usually do not appeal to everyone.

Consider the income potential of each segment carefully when defining segments.
When defining segments consider:
1. Can you measure the segment?.
2. Is the segment big enough to make a profit?
3. Is the segment changing or evolving?
4. Can you reach the segment?
5. Is there one factor that unites everyone in the segment?
6. Do you have enough data to understand the segment?

PERSONAS

WHAT ARE PERSONAS ?
"A persona is a archetypal character that is meant to represent a group of users in a role who share common goals, attitudes and behaviors when interacting with a particular product or service Personas are user models that are presented as specific individual humans. They are not actual people, but are synthesized directly from observations of real people."(Cooper)

WHO INVENTED IT?
Alan Cooper 1998

WHY USE THIS METHOD?
1. Helps create empathy for users and reduces self reference.
2. Use as tool to analyze and gain insight into users.
3. Help in gaining buy-in from stakeholders.

HOW TO USE THIS METHOD
1. Inaccurate personas can lead to a false understandings of the end users. Personas need to be created using data from real users.
2. Collect data through observation, interviews, ethnography.
3. Segment the users or customers
4. Create the Personas
5. Avoid Stereotypes
6. Each persona should be different. Avoid fringe characteristics. Personas should each have three to four life goals which are personal aspirations,
7. Personas are given a name, and photograph.
8. Design personas can be followed by building customer journeys

RESOURCES
Raw data on users from interviews or other research
Images of people similar to segmented customers.
Computer
Graphics software

PERSONA TEMPLATE

PHOTO OF PERSONA

PERSONA NAME

Age
Occupation
Location

Income
Gender
Education

CHARACTERISTICS

GOALS

What does this person want to achieve in life?

MOTIVATIONS

Incentives
Fear
Growth

Achievement
Power
Social

FRUSTRATIONS

What experiences does this person wish to avoid?

QUOTE

Characteristic quote

BRANDS

What brands does this persona purchase or wish to purchase?

CHARACTERISTICS

• • • • • • • • • • • • • • • • • • • •

EXTROVERT   INTROVERT   FREE TIME

• • • • • • • • • • • • • • • • • • • •

TRAVEL   LUXURY GOODS

• • • • • • • • • • • • • • • • • • • •

TECHNICAL SAVVY   SPORTS

• • • • • • • • • • • • • • • • • • • •

SOCIAL NETWORKING   MOBILE APPS

POINT OF VIEW STATEMENT

End user:

....

Needs to:

....

Because [your insight]:

....

REFRAMING THE PROBLEM

WHAT IS IT?
This method helps develop innovative solutions with a number of questions.

WHO INVENTED IT?
Tudor Rickards 1974 Manchester Business School

WHY USE THIS METHOD?
1. To create different perspectives and new ideas.

RESOURCES
1. Pen
2. Paper
3. White board
4. Dry Erase markers

HOW TO USE THIS METHOD
1. Define the problem that you would like to address.

Complete these sentences while considering your problem.
1. "There is more than one way of looking at a problem. You could also define this problem in another way as."
2. "The underlying reason for the problem is."
3. "I think that the best solution is."
4. "If I could break all laws of reality I would try to solve it by."
5. "You could compare this problem to the problem of."
6. "Another, different way of thinking about it is"

REFRAMING MATRIX

PRODUCT

1. Is there something wrong with the product or service?
2. Is it priced correctly?
3. How well does it serve the market?
4. Is it reliable?

PLANNING

1. Are our business plans, marketing plans, or strategy at fault?
2. Could we improve these?

POTENTIAL

1. How would we increase sales?
2. If we were to seriously increase our targets or our production volumes, what would happen with this problem?

PEOPLE

1. What are the people impacts and people implications of the problem?
2. What do people involved with the problem think?
3. Why are customers not buying the product?

DESIGN PROBLEM ....

....

....

....

....

....

....

....

REFRAMING MATRIX

WHAT IS IT?
The reframing matrix is a method of approaching a problem by imagining the perspectives of a number of different people and exploring the possible solutions that they might suggest.

WHO INVENTED IT?
Michael Morgan 1993

WHY USE THIS METHOD?
This is a method for assisting in empathy which is an important factor in gaining acceptance and creating successful design.

CHALLENGES
The reframing is not done with stakeholders present or in context so may be subjective

RESOURCES
Pens
Paper
Post it notes
White board
Dry erase markers

HOW TO USE THIS METHOD
1. Define a problem.
2. On a white board or paper draw a large square and divide it into four quadrants.
3. Select 4 different perspectives to approach the problem. They could be four professions or four people or four other perspectives that are important for your problem.
4. With your team brainstorm a number of questions that you believe are important from the perspectives that you have selected.
5. The moderator writes the questions in the relevant quadrants of the matrix.
6. The group discusses each of these questions.
7. The answers are recorded and the perspectives are incorporated into the considerations for design solutions.

LOW-FIDELITY PROTOTYPING

WHAT IS IT?
Low-fi prototyping is a quick and cheap way of gaining insight and informing decision-making without the need for costly investment. Simulates function but not aesthetics of proposed design. Prototypes help compare alternatives and help answer questions about interactions or experiences.

WHY USE THIS METHOD?
1. May provide the proof of concept
2. It is physical and visible
3. Inexpensive and fast.
4. Useful for refining functional and perceptual interactions.
5. Assists to identify any problems with the design.
6. Helps to reduce the risks
7. Helps members of team to be in alignment on an idea.
8. Helps make abstract ideas concrete.
9. Feedback can be gained from the user

CHALLENGES
A beautiful prototype completed too early can stand in the way of finding the best design solution.

HOW TO USE THIS METHOD
1. Construct models, not illustrations
2. Select the important tasks, interactions or experiences to be prototyped.
3. Build to understand problems.
4. If it is beautiful you have invested too much.
5. Make it simple
6. Assemble a kit of inexpensive materials
7. Preparing for a test
8. Select users
9. Conduct test
10. Record notes on the 8x5 cards.
11. Evaluate the results
12. Iterate

RESOURCES
Paper
Cardboard
Wire
Foam board,
Post-it-notes
Hot melt glue

APPEARANCE PROTOTYPE

WHAT IS IT?
Appearance prototypes look like but do not work like the final product. The are often fabricated using a variety of rapid prototyping techniques from digital 3d models or by hand in materials such as hard foam, wood or plastics. Usually, appearance prototypes are "for show" and short term use and are not designed to be handled.

CHALLENGES
1. Designers can become too attached to their prototypes and allow them to become jewelry that stands in the way of further refinement.
2. Clients may believe that the design is finalized when more refinement is required.
3. They are expensive to produce,

WHY USE THIS METHOD?
May be used to get approval for a final design from a client or to create images for literature or a web site prior to the availability of manufactured products.

HOW TO USE THIS METHOD
1. They give non-designers a good idea of what the production object will look like and feel like.

TEST PLAN

SCOPE
Indicate what you are testing Specify how much of the service the test will cover.

PURPOSE
Identify the concerns, questions, and goals for this test. These can be quite broad or specific Identify your focus. Base your test scenarios on your gaols and focus.

SCHEDULE & LOCATION
Indicate when and where you will do the test. How many sessions and when will they be held?

SESSIONS
Describe the sessions, sessions are often 60 to 90 minutes. Allow 30 minutes contingency between sessions.

EQUIPMENT
Computer, phone,. Are you planning on recording the session?

PARTICIPANTS
1. Number and types of participants to be tested you will be recruiting.
2. How will they be recruited?
3. Screener.

SCENARIOS
Number and types of tasks included in testing.
For a 60 min. test, you should have 10 (+/-2) scenarios for desktop or laptop testing and 8 (+/- 2) scenarios for a mobile/smartphone test. Include more in the test plan so the team can choose the appropriate tasks.

METRICS
Subjective metrics Include the questions you are going to ask the participants prior to the sessions

QUANTITATIVE METRICS
Successful completion rates, error rates, time on task.

ROLES
A list of the staff involvedin the usability testing and what role each will play.

SMART GOALS

What are your goals?
Answer the following questions

Specific
What will you design?

Measurable
How will you know when you have the best solution.
How will you measure progress toward your goal?

Attainable
Is your goal a possible to achieve with your time and resources?

Realistic
Is your goal realistic and within your reach? Are you willing to commit to your goal?

Relevant
Is your goal relevant to your long term needs?

Time
What is your target time-frame to reach the gaols?

ITERATION QUESTIONS

Modify and improve your prototype based on your previous feedback. Show it to five people and answer the following questions.

What works in the design?

1.

2.

3

4.

What doesn't work in the design?

1.

2.

3.

4.

What refinements need to be made?

1.

2.

3.

4.

SAMPLE INTERVIEW CONSENT FORM

Research should, be based on participants' freely volunteered informed consent. The researcher has a responsibility to explain what the research is about and who will see the data. Participants should be aware that they can refuse to participate; confidentiality, and how the research will be used.

The information contained within this book is strictly for educational purposes. If you wish to apply ideas contained in this book you are taking full responsibility for your actions. There are no representations or warranties, express or implied, about the completeness, accuracy, reliability, suitability or availability with respect to the information, products, services, or related graphics contained in this book for any purpose. Any use of this information is at your own risk.

Purpose of the research
The purpose of this project is [purpose]. *Provide a brief, usually one-paragraph, explanation of what the research is about and state why the subject is being asked to participate [e.g., inclusion/exclusion criteria]*

What we will ask you to do
If you agree to be in this study, you are asked to participate in a recorded interview. The interview will include questions about [topic] , The interview will take about [duration] minutes to complete. With your permission, we would also like to tape-record the interview.

Risks and benefits
There is the risk that you may find some of the questions about [topic] to be sensitive. *[Describe any possible benefit to the participants or others that may reasonably be expected from the research; then describe any reasonably foreseeable risks or discomforts to the participants, or state "there are no foreseeable risks," if none are identified.]*

Compensation:
There will be [amount of compensation] [type of compensation] compensation. *[Specify whether participants will be compensated and if so, the amount. If amount will be prorated for any reason, state this.]*

Taking part is voluntary
Taking part in this interview is completely voluntary. You may skip any questions that you do not want to answer. If you decide not to take part or to skip some of the questions, it will not affect your current or future relationship with Cornell University. If you decide to take part, you are free to withdraw at any time.

Your answers will be confidential
The records of this project will be kept private. In any sort of report we make public we will not include any information that will make it possible to identify you. Research records will be kept in a locked file; only [who] will have access to the records. [Regarding the storage of the tape, who will keep it, where will it be stored, after the transcription is done?] If we tape-record the interview, we will destroy the tape after it has been transcribed, which we anticipate will be within [duration] months of its taping.
If you have questions: [contact]

If you have questions
The researchers conducting this study are [researchers]. Please ask any questions you have now. If you have questions later, you may contact [name] at [email] or at [phone].

Statement of Consent
I have read the above information, and have received answers to any questions I asked. I consent to take part in the project. In addition to agreeing to participate, I also consent to having the interview tape-recorded. I understand the information presented above and that: My participation is voluntary, and I may withdraw my consent and discontinue participation in the project at any time. My refusal to participate will not result in any penalty.

You will be given a copy of this form to keep for your records.

Interviewee Signature ....Date ....
In addition to agreeing to participate, I also consent to having the interview tape-recorded.

Researcher's Signature ....Date ....
This consent form will be kept by the researcher for at least [duration] years beyond the end of the project and was approved by the [Organization] on [date].

This consent form will be kept by the researcher for at least [duration] years beyond the end of the project and was approved by the [Organization] on [date].

TESTING SCRIPTS

RECRUITMENT SCRIPT
Hello, may I speak with X We are looking for participants to take part in a research study evaluating the usability of the X Product. There will be $xx payment for the hour long session, which will take the X Building located downtown. The session would involve one-on-one meeting with a researcher where you would sit down in front of a computer and try to use a product while being observed and answering
questions about the product. Would you be interested in participating? If not: Thank you for taking the time to speak with me. If you know of anyone else who might be interested in participating please have them call me, at xxx-xxx-xxxx

SCREENING SCRIPT
I need to ask you a couple of questions to determine whether you meet the eligibility criteria— Do you have a couple of minutes? If not: When is a good time to call back? Keep in mind that your answers to these questions to not automatically allow or disallow you take part in the study—we just need accurate information about your background, so please answer as well as you can.
Have you ever used X product?
If yes:
How long have you used it for? [criteria: at least 1 yr.]
And how often do you use it? [criteria: at least 3 times a month]
If no:
Have you ever used any data processing products, such as [list competitor or similar products]? [criteria: Yes]
If yes: How long have you used it for? [criteria: at least 1 yr.]
And how often do you use it? [criteria: at least 3 times a month]
Self-identify participant gender via voice and name and other cues.

SCHEDULING
If participant meets criteria: Will you be able to come to the X Building located downtown for one hour between May 15 and 19? Free parking is available next to the building. How is [name available times and dates]? You will be participating in a one-on-one usability test session on [date and time]. Do you require any special accommodations?
I need to have an e-mail address to send specific directions and confirmation information to. Thanks again! If participant does not meet criteria: Unfortunately, you do not fit the criteria for this

particular evaluation and will not be able to participate. Thank you for taking the time to speak with me.

PARTICIPANT RECRUITMENT SCREENER

The usability test of the X Product requires 12 participants from 2 user groups.

User type experienced Product users
Number 6
Characteristics current product users/customers who have used x product
For at least 1 year and use it at least 3 times a month
3 males, 3 females

User type New product users
Number 6
Characteristics People who have no prior experience with X Product, but do have at least 1 year's experience using similar products
(e.g. data processing tools).
3 males, 3 females

THINK OUT LOAD SCRIPT

When you are doing the testing there may be times that you become frustrated or confused, but you do not say anything, We want you to say it out loud so we can see the problem and improve the design. We only can recognize what you tell us is a problem. Let us know what you are thinking. There here are no wrong answers. We're looking for your genuine impressions. Your comments will help us improve the design.

Source: Usability Testing Basics. An Overview

BENCHMARKING MATRIX FOR PRODUCT DESIGN

Criteria	A	B	C	D	E	F	G	H	I
Usability	1	2	3	1	4	1	1	2	3
Speed to market	2	1	1	2	2	4	2	1	4
Brand compatibility	2	1	1	2	2	4	2	1	4
Return on investment	2	4	0	2	2	4	0	4	4
Fits strategy	2	3	1	1	4	1	1	3	3
Aesthetic appeal	1	1	1	4	0	3	1	2	2
Differentiation	2	4	0	2	2	4	0	4	4
Tooling cost	2	2	2	0	1	1	3	3	0
Fits distribution	2	2	1	1	1	2	0	4	3
Profitable	2	2	3	1	2	1	4	0	3
Fits trends	3	3	5	3	0	3	2	1	3
Low invest	1	3	2	2	1	3	4	3	2
Total	23	27	24	20	22	27	23	25	33

BENCHMARKING

WHAT IS IT?
Benchmarking is a method for organizations to compare their products, services or customer experiences with other industry products, services and experiences to identify the best practices.

WHO INVENTED IT?
Robert Camp Xerox, 1989 Benchmarking: the search for industry best practices that lead to superior performance.

WHY USE THIS METHOD?
1. A tool to identify, and implement the best practices.
2. The practice of measuring your performance against best competitors.

CHALLENGES
1. Can be expensive
2. Organizations often think their companies were performing above the average for the industry when they are not.

HOW TO USE THIS METHOD
1. Identify what your objective.
2. Identify potential partners
3. Identify similar industries and organizations.
4. Identify organizations that are leaders.
5. Identify data sources
6. Identify the products or organizations to be benchmarked
7. Select the benchmarking factors to measure.
8. Undertake benchmarking
9. Research the "best practice" organizations
10. Analyze the outcomes
11. Target future performance
12. Adjust goal
13. Modify your own product or service to conform with best practices identified in the benchmarking process.

RESOURCES
Post-it-notes
Pens
Dry-erase markers
Whiteboard
Paper

SWOT ANALYSIS

WHAT IS IT?
SWOT Analysis is a useful technique for understanding your strengths and weaknesses, and for identifying both the opportunities open to you and the threats you face.

SWOT may be used to
- Understand your business better
- Address weaknesses
- Deter threats
- Capitalise on opportunities
- Take advantage of your strengths
- Develop business goals and strategies for achieving them.

WHO INVENTED IT?
Albert Humphrey 1965 Stanford University

WHY USE SWOT ANALYSIS?
1. SWOT analysis can help you uncover opportunities that you can exploit.
2. SWOT analyysis does not require special training or technical expertise.
3. Multi-level analysis
4. Access to a range of data from multiple sources enhances decision-making.
5. You can analysis both your own organization, product or service as well as those of competitors.
6. Helps develop a strategy of differentiation.
7. SWOT can be performed in a short time.

CHALLENGES
1. No weighting Factors
2. SWOT may be subjective.
3. May reflect the bias of individuals who participate in the brainstorming session.
4. May be hard to identify threats.

HOW TO USE THIS METHOD
1. Explain basic rules of brainstorming.
2. Ask questions related to the four SWOT categories.
3. Address Opportunities category after the other three categories.
4. Record answers on a white board or video
5. Categorize ideas into groups

RESOURCES
Post-it-notes
SWOT template
Pens
White board
Video camera
Dry-erase markers

SWOT TEMPLATE

Strengths

Weaknesses

Opportunities

Threats

SAMPLE SWOT QUESTIONS

STRENGTHS
1. Advantages of proposition
2. Capabilities
3. Competitive advantages
4. Marketing - reach, distribution
5. Innovative aspects
6. Location and geographical
7. Price, value, quality?
8. Accreditation, certifications
9. Unique selling proposition
10. Human resources
11. Experience,
12. Assets
13. Return on investment
14. Processes, IT, communications
15. Cultural, attitudinal, behavioral
16. Management cover, succession

WEAKNESSES
1. Value of proposition
2. Things we cannot do.
3. Things we are not good at
4. Perceptions of brand
5. Financial
6. Own known vulnerabilities
7. Time scales, deadlines and pressures
8. Reliability of data, plan predictability
9. Morale, commitment, leadership
10. Accreditation,
11. Cash flow, start-up cash-drain
12. Continuity, supply chain robustness

OPPORTUNITIES
1. Market developments
2. Competitors' vulnerabilities
3. New USP's
4. Tactics - surprise, major contracts
5. Business and product development
6. Information and research
7. Partnerships, agencies, distribution
8. Industrial trends
9. Technologies
10. Innovations
11. Global changes
12. Market opportunities
13. Specialized market niches
14. New exports or imports
15. Volumes, production, economies

THREATS
1. Political effects
2. Legislative effects
3. Obstacles faced
4. Insurmountable weaknesses
5. Environmental effects
6. IT developments
7. Competitor intentions
8. Loss of key staff
9. Sustainable financial backing
10. Market demand
11. New technologies, services, ideas
12. Regulations
13. Internal processes

REFRAMING MATRIX

PRODUCT PERSPECTIVE
1. Is there something wrong with the product or service?
2. Is it priced correctly?
3. How well does it serve the market?
4. Is it reliable?

PLANNING PERSPECTIVE
Are our business plans, marketing plans, or strategy at fault?
1. Could we improve these?

POTENTIAL PERSPECTIVE
1. How would we increase sales?
2. If we were to seriously increase our targets or our production volumes, what would happen with this problem?

PEOPLE PERSPECTIVE
1. What are the people impacts and people implications of the problem?
2. What do people involved with the problem think?
3. Why are customers not buying the product?

REFRAMING MATRIX

WHAT IS IT?
The reframing matrix is a method of approaching a problem by imagining the perspectives of a number of different people and exploring the possible solutions that they might suggest.

WHO INVENTED IT?
Michael Morgan 1993

WHY USE THIS METHOD?
1. This is a method for assisting in empathy which is an important factor in gaining acceptance and creating successful design.

CHALLENGES
The reframing is not done with stakeholders present or in context so may be subjective

RESOURCES
Pens
Paper
Post it notes
Whiteboard
Dry erase markers

HOW TO USE THIS METHOD
1. Define a problem.
2. On a Whiteboard or paper draw a large square and divide it into four quadrants.
3. Select 4 different perspectives to approach the problem. They could be four professions or four people or four other perspectives that are important for your problem.
4. With your team brainstorm a number of questions that you believe are important from the perspectives that you have selected.
5. The moderator writes the questions in the relevant quadrants of the matrix.
6. The group discusses each of these questions.
7. The answers are recorded and the perspectives are incorporated into the considerations for design solutions.

REFRAMING THE PROBLEM

WHAT IS IT?
This method helps develop innovative solutions with a number of questions.

WHO INVENTED IT?
Tudor Rickards 1974 Manchester Business School

WHY USE THIS METHOD?
To create different perspectives and new ideas.

RESOURCES
1. Pen
2. Paper
3. Whiteboard
4. Dry Erase markers

HOW TO USE THIS METHOD
Define the problem that you would like to address.

Complete these sentences while considering your problem. There is more than one way of looking at a problem. You could also define this problem in another way as."
1. "The underlying reason for the problem is."
2. "I think that the best solution is."
3. "If I could break all laws of reality I would try to solve it by."
4. "You could compare this problem to the problem of."
5. "Another, different way of thinking about it is"

GOAL GRID

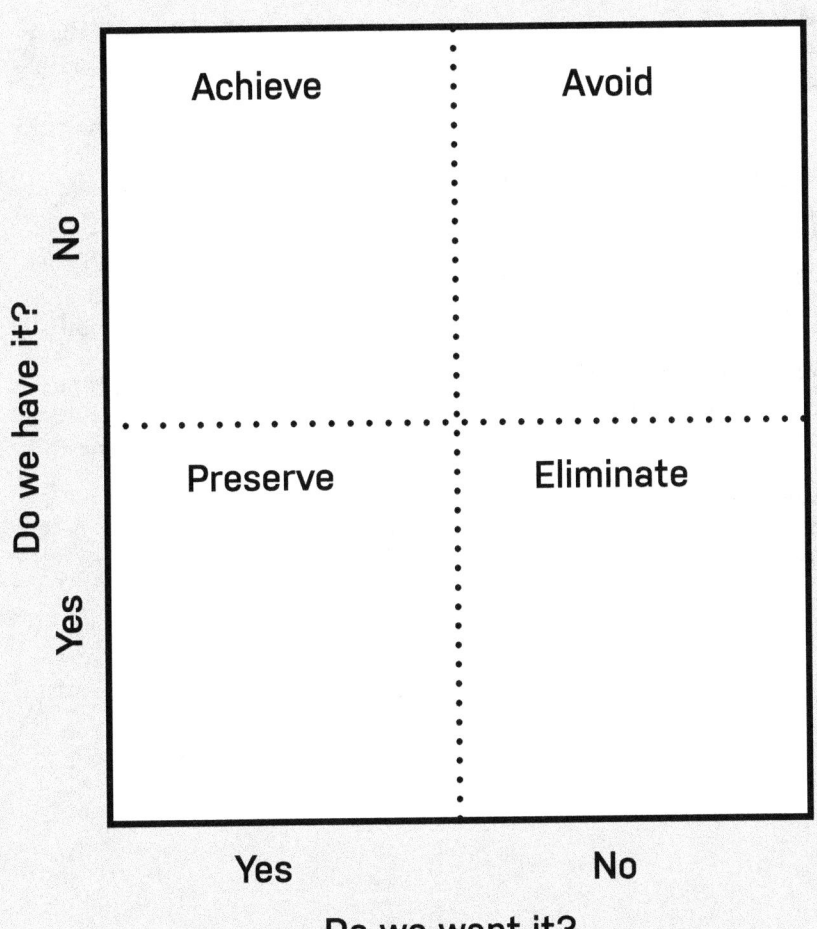

GOAL GRID

WHAT IS IT?
A goal grid is a method for clarifying goals.

"The Goals Grid also provides a structure for analyzing patterns in goals and objectives and for detecting potential conflict with the goals and objectives of others." *Fred Nickols*

WHO INVENTED IT?
Ray Forbes, John Arnold and Fred Nickols 1992

WHY USE THIS METHOD?
A goal grid is a method for clarifying goals.

HOW TO USE THIS METHOD
1. The team brainstorms a list of goals.
2. The moderator asks the team these questions:
   - "Do we have it?"
   - "Do we want it?"
   - "What are we trying to achieve?"
   - "What are we trying to preserve?"
   - "What are we trying to avoid?"
   - "What are we trying to eliminate?"

RESOURCES
Pen
Paper
Whiteboard
Dry erase markers
Post-it notes.

COMMUNICATIONS MAP

WHAT IS IT?
A communications map is a tool to study and create the strategy for communications. It may be used in a project to understand where there are gaps which could affect the project outcomes.
The project communication map documents the critical links among people and information that are necessary for successful project outcomes.

WHY USE THIS METHOD?
1. It may show where there are gaps in communications which need to be addressed.
2. Assists the project team to provide timely and accurate information to all stakeholders.

HOW TO USE THIS METHOD
1. Identify stakeholders.
2. Identify those with whom your organization needs the strongest communications linkages to.
3. Identify Internal audiences.
4. Identify peer groups or sub groups.
5. Identify strong and frequent communications
6. Identify connectivity needed to a primary audience.
7. Identify less frequent communications connectivity needed to a secondary audience.
8. Determine stakeholder needs.
9. Identify communication methods and resources.
10. Prepare communication map showing existing and desired communications.
11. Distribute to stakeholders for feedback.
12. Incorporate Changes
13. Implement.

RESOURCES
Pens
Paper
Whiteboard
Dry-erase markers
Internet connection to a network of stakeholders

RESEARCH PLAN

One of the more common questions that designer's ask when they are first doing research consulting is "How do you convince a company that they need to do research if they haven't done it before?"

I ask my clients "What do we need to know to make this project a success?"

Summarize your research approach as concisely as possible in one or two pages so that busy readers can quickly understand why you are undertaking the research and how it will be done.

RESEARCH GOALS
Your research goals, with specific questions you are trying to answer. What are the challenges you are looking to address? Why should we do this research?

RESEARCH REVIEW
Reference to existing relevant research findings and why you need additional research efforts. What questions are not answered well enough by existing research?

PARTICIPANTS AND RECRUITING
What groups of stakeholders or internal staff you are doing research with, along with privacy considerations and how you will recruit participants. Recruiting is often overlooked during initial research conversations, but it is a crucial effort that can delay a project significantly if it is not considered early in the overall process.

RESEARCH APPROACH
Your research approach, including your planned methods, analysis, and deliverables. This is the core of your research plan. Depending on your audience you may want to include more or less detail in this section.

RESOURCES
Resources that are required for this approach. What is the general need for talent, time and budget for this project? At a high level, who is involved and how? Is travel involved? Who will support recruiting, scheduling and travel logistics? Are there partners contributing to the research effort? Identify roles and individual contacts.

RESEARCH REPORTING
Research reporting, including how you will share your findings and with whom. Reference your deliverables
and establish expectations for format (written report, highlight video, presentation, etc.).

NEXT STEPS
What you need to get started with your research efforts. Identify actions and any possible issues or questions (e.g., privacy impact assessments or other legal opinion, etc.).

APPENDIX: LOGISTICS
1. Recruiting Screener – the qualifications or filters to choose participants
2. Research Guides – interview outlines or scripts. List the questions you will be asking in the interview.
3. Consent forms and procedures, including incentive receipt procedures if relevant. Recording and transcription procedures.

Source: UX toolbox government of British Columbia

A research plan is a research proposal that explains the research that you plan to do, why it is necessary, who you will study, how long it will take and how you will do it. It is often a short document of one or two pages but can be longer.

BUSINESS CASE

This is the structure of a business case. Write one sentence to one paragraph under each section heading explaining the business case for your project.

COVER PAGE
1. Project Name
2. Team Name
3. Date
4. Version
5. Submitted by:
6. Key stakeholders

EXECUTIVE SUMMARY
1. Introduction
2. State the purpose.
3. Description
4. Short description of the business.
5. Market Overview
6. Assumptions
7. Financials
8. Capital expenditures would be between
9. Revenue
    - Q2 20XX
    - Q3 20XX
    - Q4 20XX
    - Q1 20XX

1. Profit
2. Background
3. Brief statement of the needs, desires, fears and concerns.
4. The problem or need.
5. Proposed solution
6. Therefore, we are requesting funding of between $XXX and $XXX for capital and $XXX for expenses for this year and the next year for this project.
7. Strategic Fit
8. Why should the company invest into this business?
9. Market Assessment
10. Why is now the right time?
11. Project Plan
12. How will the product be built? Timelines?
13. Assumptions and Financials
14. All assumptions made and the financial implications.
15. Questions and Implementation
16. Open questions and FAQs.
17. Risk Analysis
18. What are the risks? How do you plan to mitigate the risks?
19. Conclusion and Recommendation
20. Conclude by stating what is needed and the recommendations you make.

TEST PLAN

Create a one to two page document that gives your client the following information in concise form.

SCOPE
Indicate what you are testing Specify how much of the service the test will cover.

PURPOSE
Identify the concerns, questions, and goals for this test. These can be quite broad or specific Identify your focus. Base your test scenarios on your gaols and focus.

SCHEDULE & LOCATION
Indicate when and where you will do the test. How many sessions and when will they be held?

SESSIONS
Describe the sessions, sessions are often 60 to 90 minutes. Allow 30 minutes contingency between sessions.

EQUIPMENT
Computer, phone,. Are you planning on recording the session?

PARTICIPANTS
1. Number and types of participants to be tested you will be recruiting.
2. How will they be recruited?
3. Screener.

SCENARIOS
Number and types of tasks included in testing.
For a 60 min. test, you should have 10 (+/-2) scenarios for desktop or laptop testing and 8 (+/- 2) scenarios for a mobile/smartphone test. Include more in the test plan so the team can choose the appropriate tasks.

METRICS
Subjective metrics Include the questions you are going to ask the participants prior to the sessions

QUANTITATIVE METRICS
Successful completion rates, error rates, time on task.

ROLES
A list of the staff involvedin the usability testing and what role each will play.

ERNEST HEMINGWAY'S TOP 4 TIPS FOR SUCCESSFUL WRITING

Ernest Hemingway had a simple direct writing style that dispensed with unnecessary fat and got straight to the point.

These are Hemingway's rules

1. Use short sentences.
Hemingway was challenged to tell a story in 6 words
"For sale: baby shoes, never worn."
2. Use short first paragraphs
3. Use vigorous English
Use strong, forceful, vital language that communicates passion, focus and intention. Use words that create vivid pictures in the mind of your reader that they can easily relate to
4. Be positive, not negative
Instead of saying "inexpensive," say "economical,"Instead of saying "painless," say "little discomfort"

DESIGN THINKING IS ABOUT CHANGING FROM: MAKING PEOPLE WANT THINGS [THROUGH ADVERTISING AND MARKETING] TO MAKING THINGS PEOPLE WANT

PIETER BAERT
Consutant

08
USER PROFILE CHECKLIST

USER PROFILE

DEFINE YOUR TARGET AUDIENCE
Creating a projected user models will keep the development team rooted to a realistic user requirements and minimizes user frustration with the real product. Having a deep understanding of users can help development team better understand the wants & needs of the targeted customers. This will help the development team relate better with the target user. Understanding user tasks helps in developing design solutions that will ensure that the user expectations are met & avoid design errors and customer frustration.

Use research methods such as interviewing, observation, empathy maps and user experience maps to better understand your audience.

The segmentation is carried out by using one of the five strategies

1. Behavior segmentation
2. Benefit segmentation
3. Psychographic segmentation
4. Geographic segmentation
5. Demographic segmentation

1. What is your target' groups goals emotions, experiences, needs and desires?
2. Information collected from just a few people is unlikely to be representative of the whole range of users.
3. What are the user tasks and activities?
4. How will the user use the product or service to perform a task?

Market segmentation is basically the division of market into smaller segments. It helps identify potential customers and target them.

5. What is the context of the user?
6. Where are they? What surrounds them physically and virtually or culturally?
7. How large is your user group?

SEGMENTATION
Market segmentation helps to focus on groups of customers most likely to purchase the products and services being designed.

Traditionally market segments are identified using factors such as demographics, psychographics, behavioral activities, technical knowledge, different usage and purchase situations, benefits sought from the product, usage rates, or geographic area.

REQUIREMENTS FOR SEGMENTATION
The particular segment should be:
1. Measurable
2. Accessible
3. Substantial
4. Actionable

USER PROFILE

Geographic location

Region

Urban, town or rural?

Which city of town?

City or town population range

Demographic

Gender

Age range

Race

Life Stage / Infant / Child Youth / Adult / Senior /

Birth Era / Baby boomer / 49-64 / Gen X 65-76 / Gen Y 77-94 / Gen Z 95-12 /

Household Size / 1 / 2 / 3-4 / 5-6 / 6+ /

Tenure / Own home / Rent Home /

Marital Status / Never Married / Married / Separated / Divorced / Widowed /

User profile checklist

Socioeconomic

Income Range / Less than $15,000 / 15K- 25K / 25K-35K / 35K-50K / 50K-75K / 75K-100K / 100K+

Education / Some School / Graduated High School / Some College / Graduated College/ Postgrad /

Occupation

Psychographic

Lifestyle / Activities / Interests /

Values Actualizers / fulfilleds / achievers / experiencers / believers / strivers / makers / strugglers

Personality /compulsive / social / introverted / extroverted / agressive / ambitious / etc

Culture

Purchasing behavior

Outlet type /department / specialty / outlet / convenience / supermarket / big box / catalogue / etc

Benefits Sought Quality / service / price / value / financing / warramnty / etc

Usage / Light / medium / heavy / nonuser / ex-user / prospect / novice/ first time /
regular/ expert /

Awareness / unaware/ aware / informed / interested / intending to buy / purchaser / rejected /

**KNOW YOUR BENEFITS
SELL YOUR BENEFITS**

09
PERSONA CHECKLIST

PERSONA CHECKLIST

WHAT ARE PERSONAS?
"A persona is a archetypal character that is meant to represent a group of users in a role who share common goals, attitudes and behaviors when interacting with a particular product or service. Personas are user models that are presented as specific individual humans. They are not actual people, but are synthesized directly from observations of real people."(Cooper)
The technique was developed by Alan Cooper in 1983.

WHY USE PERSONAS?
1. Helps create empathy for users and reduces self reference.
2. Use as tool to analyze and gain insight into users.
3. Help in gaining buy-in from stakeholders.

HOW TO CREATE A PERSONA
1. Inaccurate personas can lead to a false understandings of the end users. Personas need to be created using data from real users.
2. Collect data through observation, interviews, ethnography.
3. Segment the users or customers
4. Create the Personas
5. Avoid Stereotypes
6. Each persona should be different. Avoid fringe characteristics. Personas should each have three to four life goals which are personal aspirations,
7. Personas are given a name, and photograph.
8. Design personas can be followed by building customer journeys

Persona Checklist

Likes

What makes them happy?

....

What is attractive to them?

....

What are their interests and hobbies?

....

What type of people do they like?

....

What would the character like to be doing today?

....

What would the character like to be doing in five years?

....

What would the character like to be doing in ten years?

....

What would the character most like to experience?

....

What would the character most like to learn?

....

What does your customer desire?

....

What are the character's habits?

....

What does your persona need?

....

What's important to them?

....

What are their key responsibilities?

....

What are their values?

....

Dislikes

What does the character find most irritating?

....

What are the character's biases?

....

What obstacles stand between the persona and what they want or need to achieve?

....

What triggers an emotional response from the character?

....

What's their number one concern?

....

Where is the persona most unhappy?

....

What are their fears? What do they worry about?

....

What are his biggest frustrations?

....

When is your customer most unhappy?

Flaws

What are their bad habits?

....

What environmental factors will the product be exposed to? Temperature? Humidity? Loading?

....

What is the required product shelf life?

....

What problems may arise in the distribution of the product?

....

Which means of transport are used?

....

What temperatures will the product be exposed to?

....

Technology

How adept are they at using technology?

....

Are they a fluent Internet user?

....

What operating system do they use?

....

What Internet browser do they use?

....

Which is their preferred search engine?

....

Do they use any social media websites?

....

Which social media do they use?

....

What's their preferred method of communication?

....

Do they shop on-line?

....

Which websites do they usually buy from?

....

What cell phone do they use?

....

Do they prefer to pay by card or with cash?

....

What blogs do they read?

....

....

Other questions

Are they considering a career change?

....

Which political party do they support?

....

Are they environmentally conscious?

....

Which news sources do they read?

....

Do they have any children?

....

Do they exercise regularly?

....

What do they read?

....

Do they regularly go vacations?

....

Where do they go?

....

Are they a risk taker?

....

Are they introverted or extroverted?

....

Do they adapt easily to change?

....

How would their friends describe them?

....

How spontaneous are they?

....

How much do they earn?

....

HE WHO CHOOSES THE BEGINNING OF THE ROAD CHOOSES THE PLACE IT LEADS TO. IT IS THE MEANS THAT DETERMINES THE END

HARRY EMERSON FOSDICK
American Pastor

10
PRODUCT DESIGN
BRIEFING CHECKLIST

PRODUCT DESIGN BRIEFING CHECKLIST

The foundation of design project is the design brief. An effective design brief should give the design team all the information that they need to design a successful product. The esign brief should be completed before your project starts. At the start of a project an inexperienced client will sometimes say "I'm not sure what I want, I will tell you when I see something that I like". It is the designer's responsibility to define the scope of the project with the client .

A design brief prompts will reveal important background information about the client's business, as well as well as the client goals for the new product design. You will not need an answer for ever question but the more information that a designer has the more efficiently a project will run with less rework necessary.

The following questions in this section will help a designer prepare a proposal and a client to prepare an effective brief. Some of the more importanat questionsinclude:

1. The client's business's vision, mission and values
2. The client organization's products & services and how they are sold and distributed.
3. The product'sunique selling point .
4. The unmet user need that you are addressing.
5. Your ideal client profile or target audience .
6. The main competitors, and how they aare differentiated
7. The client's business goals in the next 1-2 years and 5-10 years
8. The design directions that the client definitely does not want.

Product design briefing checklist

Key Personnel

Project Manager

Design & Packaging

Research & Testing

Engineering & Human Factors

Business

Who will be the primary client point of contact?

Human factors

Marketing

Legal & Intellectual Property

Prototyping/ Modelmaking

Resources

Does the company have the financial resources?

Is the schedule realistic?

Do we have the skills needed?

General

Who is the target audience or intended market?

Who are the primary stakeholders?

What unmet user need is this product addressing?

Why is the product being developed?

What are the product performance requirements?

How will the product be differentiated?

What are the product features?

What is the desired date of market introduction?

What is the Product name & model number?

How will the product be differentiated?

Is the product part of a family?

What are the design attributes?

Are there related products or services?

260

Competitors

Please list 3 or 4 that you Like. Explain

Please list 3 or 4 products that you do not like. Explain

What competitive advantage will draw clients to your products?

Identify your competitors' URLs

Who are your top 3 or 4 competitors?

What are the competitor's web site urls?

What products or services do competitors offer and how do they compare to yours?

What media are your most successful competitors using?

Have you formally researched your competitors?.

What is it about other products that you like?

List 3 or 4 products where you like the color scheme

List 3 or 4 productswhere you like the usability

List 3 or 4 products designed for same target audience

List 3 or 4 products where you like the performance

Product design briefing checklist

How can you justify a higher price than your competitors?

If you were a customer, which of the competing products would you buy? Explain.

What are the strengths of each competor?

What are the weaknesses of each competitor?

What is the market share of each competitor?

What will be the "draw" from competitor products?

What do you do that competitors don't do?

Why should a customer obtain products and services from your website?

What are the top 3 most competitive keywords for your industry?

What are your competitor's prices?

Who may be future competitors?

Engineering & Technical

What are the performance goals?

What are the preferred materials?

What are the preferred manufacturing processes?

What will be the levels of UV exposure?

What is the required functionality?

What is the mean time between failure.

What are the design constraints?

Which components will be purchased?

What are the interface requirements?

What are the connectivity requirements?

How much power will the product use?

What are the applicable standards?

What chemicals will the product be exposed to in use?

What software platforms will be used?

Manufacturing

What will be the materials?

What will be the manufacturing processes?

What production facilities are available or preferred?

Are there preferred external suppliers?

Have all suppliers have been selected and qualified?

Is one company capable of making the whole product?

What quality standards do the manufacturers conform to?

What are the manufacturing lead times?

What are the annual projected quantities?

What are the batch sizes of components?

Which parts of this product can be purchased?

Do we need to introduce new manufacturing processes?

What are the manufacturing lead times?

Administration

How will you ensure prompt payments?

What will be your system for tracking drawings and issues?

Will you need a translator?

How will you communicate with your client?

Color

Who will be responsible for color definition?

Is there a customer preference for particular colors?

What are the brand colors? Identity? Products? Web?

Is there an existing corporate identity style manual?

What are the market trends in colors?

What are the color preferences in intended markets?

Will the chosen colors work in most contexts?

Is the logo artwork available?

Packaging

Are there packaging weight restrictions?

Are there packaging size restrictions?

Preferred packaging materials.

How many products will be packaged together?

How will packaging be displayed at point of sale?

Does the package need to be resealed?

What are the packaging performance requirements?

What bulk packaging will be required?

Which markets will the product be distributed in?

Will there be an instruction manual?

What information needs to be displayed on the packaging?

What environments will packaging be exposed to?

Will tracking information be required on packaging such as batch ID universal code or date?

Usability

How will the product be used?

Where will the product be used?

What is the operation sequence?

Who will use the product?

Who are the stakeholders

Are there problem areas for users or other stakeholders?

Does the design accommodate a range of literacy and skills?

Does the design accommodate right- or left-handed use?

Does the design minimize hazards and errors?

Does the design cater to both inexperienced users?

Is the design unnecessarily complex?

Is necessary information legible?

Is the product easy to use?

Have operational specifications been defined?

Have the users used a similar product?

Is the design consistent with user expectations?

Is the design fail-safe?

What are the range of anthropometric sizes of users?

What is the gender of users?

What is the age range of users?

How might the product be misused?

What other products will be used with this product?

Does the design provide help and documentation?

Does the design provide for privacy, security, and safety?

Does the design provide effective prompting and feedback?

Does the design follow consistency and standards?

How might the product fail in use?

Environment of Use

What impact will the product have on its environment?

What is the operating humidity range for this product?

What is the operating temperature range for this product?

What will be the level of exposure to ultraviolet light?

Are the materials identifiable?

What will be the service life of the product?

How will the product be disposed of?

Is waste generated? What type of waste is generated?

What are the energy requirements of the product?

Are materials recyclable?

Are the most environmentally friendly materials being used?

Are there hazardous materials? How will they be disposed?

Can parts be disassembled?

Research

How will we plan to fill the gaps in our knowledge?

What are our user's needs?

What information do we need to make the design succeed?

What are the gaols of research?

Who will conduct the research?

What research methods will be used?

What questions will we answer with the research?

Who will we recruit for the research?

How many participants will be recruited?

Where and when will the research be conducted?

Do we have sufficient resources for the research?

Who will analyze the research?

When will the findings be available? How will the findings be communicated and distributed?

Marketing

Is there a market for this product? How do you know?

What is the market size?

Which market segments does this product target?

How and where do your intended customers purchase?

What is the product positioning strategy?

Why will a customer purchase this product?

Does the product fit product strategy and portfolio?

How will the product be scaled for features and function?

How will the product be launched?

How will the product blend with existing products?

What are 6 most significant competitive brands and products?

Which of the competing products would you buy? Why?

Is the potential market sufficiently large to justify investment in a new product?

How will you promote and market the product?

What are the client's brand attributes?

What are the market trends that may impact this product?

What are the strengths of competing products?

What are the weaknesses of competing products?

What differentiates your company from the competition?

What is the expected life of the product in the market?

What is the strategy for collateral?

What market research has been undertaken for this product?

What will be the product story?

Where are you potential customers?

Who may be future competitors?

Will this product cannibalize existing products?

Who is the best contact for sales related questions?

Who is the best contact for marketing related questions?

Business

What are the capital requirements for the project?

Does the company have the financial resources?

Does the development team have sufficient technical, marketing, and finance expertise?

Does the pricing offer good profit margins?

Does the product fit with current strategy, and competencies?

Have the business risks been assessed

How well does the product fit with product portfolio?

How long will customers take to pay?

How many products will you need to sell to break even?

How will the product blend with existing products?

How will geographic location of end user affect profits?

How will you keep financial records?

What market research do you have?

What are the financial objectives?

What are the key risks?

What is the estimated payback period?

What is the firm's competitive advantages?

What is the return on investment ROI potential for project?

What will be the cash flow requirements to keep the business running?

What will be the trade price?

What will be the retail price?

Will there be agent's fees?

How long will customers take to pay?

Can there be subsequent add-on products?

What is the firm's company vision, strategic intent, and mission statement?

Is there support from top management?

Who is the best contact for business related questions?

Distribution

How will the product be distributed?

Does packaging design make product easily handled for transportation?

Does the design nest for transport?

How will the product be distributed nationally?

How will the product be stored?

Is the transportation as efficient as possible?

What are the optimum sizes for transport?

What chemicals will the product be exposed to?

What environmental factors will the product be exposed to? Temperature? Humidity? Loading?

What is the required product shelf life?

What problems may arise in the distribution of the product?

Which means of transport are used?

What temperatures will the product be exposed to?

Product design briefing checklist **275**

Regulatory

Local

State

National

International

Labeling requirements

Materials

Environmental

Maintenance

Who will conduct the maintenance?

How often will maintenance be required?

How will maintenance information be communicated?

What maintenance is needed?

What is the maintenance process?

Where will maintenance be done?

THE RELATIONSHIP WITH A CLIENT MUST BE 'WE.'

BILLY BALDWIN
Actor

11
BUSINESS MODEL CHECKLIST

BUSINESS MODEL CHECKLIST

The Business Model Canvas is a strategic management technique for developing new product business models. The elements make up a product's value proposition, infrastructure, customers, and finances. This technique is used by millions of people in companies of all sizes. You can use these questions to consider a new design, challenge, and build your business model. The Business Model Canvas was initially proposed by Alexander Osterwalder in 2008, based on discussions with hundreds of successful startup organizations and the planning information that they build when developing a new busines, product or service.

BUSINESS MODEL CHECKLIST

INFRASTRUCTURE

KEY ACTIVITIES
The most important activities in executing a company's value proposition.

KEY RESOURCES
The resources that are necessary to create value for the customer in order to sustain and support the business. These resources could be human, financial, physical and intellectual.

PARTNER NETWORK
Companies usually cultivate buyer-supplier relationships so they can focus on their core activity. Complementary business alliances may include joint ventures, strategic alliances between competitors or non-competitors.

OFFERING

VALUE PROPOSITION
How value proposition provides value may be associated with performance, customization, customer unmet needs, status, price, risk reduction, accessibility, or convenience.

The value propositions may be:
- Quantitative – price and functional efficiency
- Qualitative – improved customer experience

CUSTOMERS

CUSTOMER SEGMENTS
- The segment has to be large enough so that you can earn a profit from it.
- The segment should be stable and not reducing in size over time.
- The segment should be accessible through your marketing and sales activities.
- You need to be able to sell the product cost effectively.
- Each member of a particular segment should have one thing in common.
- Your target consumers must always respond to certain marketing actions.
- There is enough data to enable you to make informed decisions.

Customers can be segmented based on:
- Geographic segmentation
- Demographic segmentation
- Psychographic segmentation
- Behavioral segmentation

CHANNELS

A company can deliver its products to its targeted customers through different channels. Examples of channels are in-store sales, sales via Internet, or sales via mobile devices.

FINANCES

COST STRUCTURE
This is related to a company's business model.
Classes of Business Structures:
- Cost-Driven
- Value-Driven

REVENUE STREAMS
Some ways to generate a revenue stream:
- Asset Sale
- Usage Fee
- Subscription Fees
- Lending/Leasing/Renting
- Licensing

RESOURCES
The financial, human and other inputs that the company uses to create its value proposition and deliver the product to customers.

Business Model Checklist

Customer segments

Who is your customer?

....

What are the sub-segments?

....

Who is the most important customer?

....

For whom are we creating value?

Value proposition

What value do we deliver to the customer?

....

Which one of our customer's problems are we helping to solve?

....

Which customer needs are we satisfying?

....

What bundles of products and services are we offering to each Customer Segment?

Channels

Through which Channels do our Customer Segments want to be reached?

....

How are we reaching them now?

....

How are our Channels integrated?

....

Which ones work best?

Which ones are most cost-efficient?

How are we integrating them with customer routines?

Customer Relationships

What type of relationship does each of our segments expect us to maintain with them?

Which ones have we established? How costly are they?

How are they integrated with the rest of our business model?

Key Resources

What Key Resources do our Value Propositions require?

What Key Resources do our Distribution Channels require?

What Key Resources do our Customer Relationships require?

What Key Resources do our Revenue Streams require?

Key Activities

What Key Activities do our Value Propositions require?

What Key Activities do our Distribution Channels require?

What Key Activities do our Customer Relationships require?

What Key Activities do our Revenue streams require?

Key Partnerships
Who are our Key Partners?

Who are our key suppliers?

Which Key Resources are we acquiring from partners?

Which Key Activities do partners perform?

Cost Structure
What are the most important costs?

Which Key Resources are most expensive?

Which Key Activities are most expensive?

Revenue Streams
For what value are our customers really willing to pay?

Business model checklist

For what do they currently pay

How are they currently paying?

How would they prefer to pay?

How much does each revenue stream contribute to revenues?

What type of relationship does each of our segments expect us to maintain with them?

Which ones have we established? How costly are they?

How are they integrated with the rest of our business model?

Key Resources

What Key Resources do our Value Propositions require?

What Key Resources do our Distribution Channels require?

What Key Resources do our Customer Relationships require?

What Key Resources do our Revenue Streams require?

Key Activities

What Key Activities do our Value Propositions require?

Sources: Adapted from Business Model Generation by Alex Osterwalder & Yves Pigneur CC Attribution License

12
GLOSSARY

SOME TERMS USED IN PROPOSALS & LICENSING AGREEMENTS

ADD-ON
Something added to the main product to increase interest and sales in the main product.

ADJUSTED GROSS REVENUE
Royalty percentage is calculated based on the revenue left after costs such as charge backs, spoilage, damages, returns, allowances are deducted from the profits.

ADVANCE ON ROYALTIES
Payment made prior to the product going to market to the Inventor. Once the product is on the market the Inventor does not receive any royalties until the advance is equaled in royalties paying the company back for the advance.

ANGEL INVESTOR
Investor for the development and production of your product usually for a portion of ownership of the company or product.

BID
This term is normally used when a client is seeking competitive prices from several different suppliers. Many corporations have strict guidelines for the competitive bidding process.

BILL OF MATERIALS BOM
A complete list of the various materials, components, sub-components, and quantities of each component needed to manufacture the finished product.

CAD
Computer Aided Design Design generated by the designer using a computer.

CE COMMISSION OF EUROPE
The CE mark is used to certify a product has met the European Union health, safety and environmental requirements that ensure workplace and consumer safety.

COST OF GOODS COG
The total cost attributed to the production of the product sold by the company including the material and labor costs.

DISTRIBUTION CHANNEL
Manner that services or products get from the vendor to the consumer for example in-store or online sales.

EFFECTIVE DATE
The date all parties agreed the agreement comes into effect.

ELECTRICAL TESTING LAB ETL
Recognized by the Occupational Safety Health Association as a Nationally Recognized Testing Laboratory for testing products.

ESTIMATE
An estimate is tentative and non-binding. It is a projection of the approximate costs that you anticipate on a project. The total is usually described as a rough "ballpark" figure or presented as a high/low range.

EXCLUSIVITY
An agreement between the Inventor and the company stating that the company will be the only party entitled to manufacture and sell your product. It can be written for one market or all markets.

FIRST RIGHT OF REFUSAL
The designer agrees that they will offer the design to a particular company before offering it to other companies.

FREE ON BOARD
Refers to cost that the buyer pays for shipment and loading costs.

FULFILLMENT
The distribution process of moving products from the factory to the retailer, managing sales, and collection and distribution of funds.

GAP ANALYSIS
A process where you look at a particular product, its place in the market, its competitors, and study what market share and profit you could attain.

GAP IN THE MARKET
A place in the market that has potential customers and there is an unmet need. These gaps can be opportunities for companies or individuals to expand their reach into the market place.

HOLD FEE
Payment made to designer to allow company to keep your product for evaluation without the Inventor sending it to another company.

HOOK
The main feature of your product that will make a consumer see value in the product.

LANDED COST
Includes freight, insurance, port fees, purchase price and any other costs that might be incurred to bring the product to the final port of destination.

LAUNCH DATE
Date the company plans to have the product on store shelves available to consumers.

LETTER OF AGREEMENT
This is a written recap of items that have already been agreed to orally. It's a bad idea for any creative firm to begin a project solely on the basis of an oral agreement-always protect yourself by having a signed document. A letter of agreement is better than nothing, but it's smarter to submit a complete proposal.

LETTER OF INTENT
Used to state each parties intent and course of action to meet a common goal. These documents are normally followed by a formal contract between the two parties once everyone is in agreement. Letter of Intent – in most cases a LOI shows that a company is interested in moving forward towards a contract and outlines some of the terms under which they plan on proceeding.

LICENSING AGREEMENT
Document stating the terms of payment both parties agree to for licensing the product. These can include minimums, advances, royalties; payment schedule, length of contract assigned rights and whatever can be negotiated by both parties.

LINE REVIEW
The process of a company showing their product line to a retail chain in order for the retail chain to sell the products.

MANUFACTURE GROSS PROFIT The difference between the development price and the wholesale price.

MARGIN
The difference of the cost price of a product and the selling price of that product.

MARKET SHARE
The percentage share a product has of total sales within a given market.

MILESTONE
A tangible scheduled accomplishment that is met within a project.

MINIMUM ORDER QUANTITY
The minimum amount of product you have to order to get the product and the company selling to you to make a profit.

MINIMUM ROYALTY PAYMENT
The lowest amount per your contract you will receive quarterly in royalties no matter how many units of the product are sold.

NICHE MARKET
A specific segment of a largerl consumer market thst hsd a particular unifying characteristic.

NON-DISCLOSURE NDA
A document that both parties signs agreeing to keep any information discussed or shown confidential. Each party must get a signed original for their records of the document.

NON-EXCLUSIVE
An agreement that the company has the right to manufacture and sell your product, but the Inventor is still able to make the same agreement with other companies

PATENT ATTORNEY
Writes patent claims, researches the patent and works to help the client obtain a patent on their idea/product.

PATENT SEARCH
A search done by a patent attorney to see if any other patent has been issued on the same or similar concept to your design.

PERCEIVED VALUE
The value perceived by a customer that prompts them to buy one product instead of another.

PRODUCT ADAPTATION
Modifications to the existing product to improve it.

PROOF OF CONCEPT
The ability to demonstrate via a prototype, engineering model, 3-D animation, etc that your product actually will work as claimed.

PROTOTYPE MOLDS
Molds used to for prototyping short run manufacturing and used as a bridge tooling before moving to large-scale manufacturing.

QUOTE
A quote is much more precise. It is a firm offer to perform specified services for a fixed price. For example, printing companies submit quotes based on the exact specifications provided to them by clients.

Glossary

RETAIL PRICE
The price for a product or service sold to the consumer. This price is not used when calculating an Inventor's royalty rate.

RETURN ON INVESTMENT ROI
The return in profits to compared to the investment.

RUNNING ROYALTY
A royalty paid to the designer based on the number of units sold or manufactured instead of a one time lump sum.

STOCK KEEPING UNIT SKU
Every SKU is identified with its own unique number tied to a particular item. This helps track product and inventory.

TERM SHEET
A document that is used as a starting point in negotiations between two parties including licensing fee, royalties, percentages, advances, payment schedule, and milestones. Each party brings the terms that they are willing to accept.

UNDERWRITER'S LABORATORY UL
Recognized by Occupational Safety Health Association as a Nationally Recognized Testing Laboratory.

UNIT COST
Final cost to the manufacturer after adding in all of the associated costs to manufacture. including materials, manufacturing, shipping, taxes, tariffs and other costs..

WHOLESALE PRICE
The price the manufacturer charges distributers for the product. This price is what is used to base the designer's royalty percentage payment.

13
INDEX

INDEX

Symbols

3D 57, 58, 109, 129
3D sketch model 57
10 x 10 sketch method 60
.x 60

A

activities
activity 204–313
address 73, 86, 164, 227
aesthetic 98
affinity diagrams 42
age 44, 211–313
agreement 7, 2, 4, 36, 64, 119, 156, 158, 159, 160, 162, 175, 188, 189, 195, 196, 197, 202
alignment 19
alpha prototype 58
Amanda Jesnoewski 12, 13
analysis 227
analyze 210, 250
annual expenditure 13
appearance model 57
appearance prototype 58
arbitration 165
assembly concept model 57
assignments 165
audience 8, 104
authenticity 52
availability 3
awards 9, 313

B

background 18
ballpark 6, 7, 36, 172
behavior 37, 53, 62, 67, 106, 247
benchmark 44
benchmarking 226
benefits 30, 31, 32, 39, 74, 78, 90, 94, 136, 148, 170, 207, 221, 245, 248
benefits map 207
best guess 53, 173
beta prototype 58
bid 36
body text 15, 16
brainstorm 45, 215, 231
brainstorming 42, 128, 227, 311
brainstorms 234
brand 15
break-even point
brief 63, 129, 130, 239
building 210
bundling
business 229
business card 15
business mission 37
byline 16

C

camera 204
cancellation fee 10, 157
capitals 18
cards 216
challenges 216

change 7, 3, 9, 34, 52, 55, 56,
    63, 111, 155, 157, 158, 161,
    164, 175, 254
channels 208
charges 154, 155, 157, 164
client 6, 7, 2, 3, 4, 5, 6, 7, 8, 9,
    10, 11, 12, 22, 23, 24, 25,
    26, 27, 28, 29, 30, 31, 32,
    33, 34, 36, 39, 67, 73, 76,
    80, 81, 84, 85, 86, 87, 88,
    89, 90, 91, 94, 96, 97, 100,
    101, 103, 104, 106, 108,
    111, 118, 120, 122, 136, 138,
    140, 144, 146, 148, 151, 152,
    153, 154, 155, 156, 157,
    158, 159, 160, 161, 162,
    164, 165, 168, 169, 170,
    172, 174, 175, 176, 196, 197,
    198, 199, 217, 240, 257,
    258, 264, 271
client responsibilities 164
color 15, 20, 130
combining fonts 14, 16
communicate 15, 18
communication 15, 16, 20
communications 229, 235
communications map 235
competitive analysis 37
competitive products 44
competitive strategy 207
competitor analysis 105
complementary fonts 16
complex ideas 52
complex interactions 55
concept 216
concept of operation model 57

conclusions 61
conclusions and
    recommendations 61
conditions 152, 153, 162
confidentiality 76, 162, 165
conflict 234
consistency 19, 20
constraints 44, 48, 51, 104, 262
contact 3, 9, 10, 73, 74, 75, 76,
    138, 139, 145, 222
content 15, 19, 20, 29, 53, 100
context 16, 44, 47, 49, 215, 231,
    245
contingencies 63
contract 8, 13, 26, 27, 29, 118,
    152, 157, 159, 160, 161, 165,
    166, 178
contrast 16, 18, 20
convenience 3, 89
conversation 11, 54
corporations 36, 141, 145
costs 24, 30, 101, 105, 169, 194,
    199, 284
credibility 19
cross-disciplinary 3, 5, 141
culture 44, 78, 202
Curedale, Rob 308, 310, 311
customer 208, 210, 250
customers 208, 209, 210, 214,
    230, 250

D

dark horse 43
dark horse prototype 217
data 53, 61, 64, 65, 66, 106,

Index 295

112, 125, 209, 210, 221, 223, 224, 226, 227, 229, 250, 280
date 76, 77, 119, 164, 196, 197, 222, 238
day in the life 42
decorative fonts 16
defer judgment 54
deliverables 44
dependability 3
deposit 119, 166
design development model 57
designer 119, 145, 162, 164, 165, 172, 190, 196, 197, 198, 199
design hours 169
design language 15, 93
design problem 51
design process 42, 44
design thinking 44
design thinking process 44
desire 47, 68, 251
desk top walkthrough 59
diagnostic 42
Dieter Rams 98
differentiation 45, 88, 93, 227
digital camera 204
discovery phase 48, 103
discriminator 33
document 44, 45
dry-erase markers 227

E

education 50, 137, 141, 186, 211, 247
elapsed time 169

emotionally 55
empathize 42, 44
empathy 49, 79, 210, 244, 250
empathy maps 49, 79, 244
encourage wild ideas 54
end 3, 9, 27, 32, 34, 42, 43, 48, 50, 52, 53, 56, 61, 62, 64, 67, 68, 74, 78, 84, 86, 90, 94, 102, 103, 105, 107, 109, 113, 133, 135, 140, 164, 174, 205, 210, 222, 250, 255, 272
engineering 3, 5, 101, 128, 145
Ernest Hemingway 21, 241
estimate 2, 6, 10, 22, 23, 36, 75, 100, 120, 122, 169
ethnography 210, 250
evaluate 24, 45, 59, 67, 69, 103, 112
evidence based 64
exclusive 11, 24
experience 10, 12, 13, 29, 30, 34, 44, 49, 51, 52, 58, 59, 61, 74, 78, 79, 81, 95, 96, 110, 114, 116, 137, 145, 224, 244, 251, 279, 313
experience maps 49, 79, 244
experiences 211, 216
experimental prototype 58
external stakeholders 50, 128, 129

F

failpoints 56
failure 8, 27, 31, 32, 47, 68, 163,

262
feasibility prototype 59
feedback 45
fees 9, 154, 155, 158, 165, 169, 281
fidelity 45, 48, 54, 55, 56, 61, 67, 109, 110, 128, 150, 216
file formats 10
final product 55, 56, 58, 217
first samples 45
five whys 42, 202
foam model 59
focus 311
focus groups 42, 311
focus Groups 42, 311
font 15
fonts 15, 16
font size 16
font styles 15
font weight 16
Force Majeure 161, 164
foundation 7, 48, 103, 257
functional concept model 57
functionality 55, 56, 57, 262
future 205

G

gain 210, 250
Gantt, Henry 124
gender 6, 37, 44, 78, 208, 223, 267
gender, 44
generalist 33
goal 226
goal grid 234
goal map 234
goals 8, 42, 84, 205, 208, 210, 234, 250
graphics 210
gross margin 38
group 44, 208, 210, 250, 313
groups 208
gutters 19

H

headings 15, 19
headline 16
Helvetica 14, 17
Hemingway's rules 21, 241
Hermagoras of Temnos 204
heuristic 43
hierarchy 20
high-fidelity prototype 61
honest 29, 52, 98
horizontal prototyping 56
hourly rate 4, 12, 13, 25, 34, 96, 155, 157, 170, 173
how many users should you test 63
Humphrey, Albert 227

I

idea 45, 216
ideas 45, 205, 216, 227, 229
ideation 42, 54, 104, 106, 109, 121, 125
images 15, 18, 19, 20, 210
Images 18
important information 15, 20
income 6, 37, 44, 70, 78, 208,

Index 297

209
indemnity 165
industry 49, 306
information 2, 6, 2, 3, 5, 7, 9, 15, 19, 20, 32, 39, 46, 50, 51, 52, 53, 62, 65, 66, 73, 75, 76, 100, 106, 120, 138, 139, 144, 153, 155, 156, 157, 202, 204, 221, 222, 223, 235, 240, 257, 265, 266, 269, 275, 278
innovation 42, 313
innovative 98, 189, 213, 232
insight 31, 53, 54, 106, 148, 210, 212, 216, 250
insights 42, 44, 53, 54, 68, 93, 106
inspiration 68
insurance 13, 103, 162
intellectual property 45, 89, 154, 162, 190
intent 44
interactions 216
internal stakeholders 50, 128, 129
interview 44, 128, 129, 204, 221
interviews 210, 250, 311
intuitive 53
investment 216, 229
italic type 18
iterate 45
iteration 45, 67, 220

J

jargon 20, 28, 29, 39, 52, 62, 86, 94
Jon Kolko 53
Joseph Conrad

K

Kipling, Rudyard 203

L

language 15, 20, 21, 53, 62, 78, 93, 156, 157, 241
law 2, 152, 156, 157, 158, 159, 160, 165
layout 14, 15, 16, 20
legibility 18
legible 18
letter of agreement 36
license 11, 188, 190, 193, 194
long-lasting 98
lower case 18
low-fidelity prototype 61
low fidelity prototyping 216

M

manufacture 43, 45
map 207, 235
maps 208
margin for profit 13
margins 19
marital status 49
market 214, 229, 230
marketing 214, 230
market rate 12
market segmentation 37, 208
Martin, Roger 91

materials 45, 75, 130, 216
matrix 215, 231
measure 46, 61, 69, 86, 91, 113, 209, 219, 226
meeting space 13
method 42, 43, 50, 202, 204, 210, 216, 309, 310, 311
methods 208, 308
metrics 61, 113, 218, 240
mission statement 37, 273
mobility 50
moods 16
Morgan, Michael 215, 231
motivation 62

N

need 44, 51, 205, 210, 216, 235, 250
needs 6, 7, 4, 13, 28, 31, 32, 34, 39, 42, 47, 48, 49, 50, 51, 52, 53, 54, 61, 68, 72, 78, 79, 80, 86, 87, 90, 94, 103, 106, 107, 108, 137, 140, 151, 175, 205, 219, 235, 239, 244, 265, 269, 279, 282, 306
net 37
net profit 37
non-billable time 13
notes 216, 227
notices 165
not-to-exceed

O

objectives 34, 39, 45, 67, 69, 72, 80, 81, 84, 90, 101, 234, 273
observation 42, 49, 79, 150, 210, 244, 250, 311
observe 44, 51
occupation 49, 211, 247
offer 22, 23, 24, 25, 52, 192
operating expenses 32, 163
organization 227
ownership 55, 164

P

pairing fonts 16
paper 216–313
participant 62, 64, 102, 131, 223
passion 21, 241
payment 25, 153, 154, 164, 197
payments 165
pens 204
people 204, 208, 210
perceptual Maps 42
performance 44
person 208, 211
persona 42, 210, 211, 250
personal brand 15
personality 18
personalization 3
personas 210, 250
perspective 8, 50, 90, 110, 140, 144, 148
phase 24, 34, 46, 47, 48, 54, 68, 69, 96, 101, 102, 103, 104, 105, 106, 107, 108, 109, 110, 111, 113, 114, 116, 138, 139, 169

placement 15, 19
planning phase 46
point-of-view 53, 107
point of view statement 53
portfolio 6, 15, 19, 20, 28, 31, 76, 156, 158, 270, 272
position 19
positioning 37, 270
Post-it-notes 216, 227
POV 42, 53, 97, 107
pre-production 58
price 3, 22, 23, 24, 25, 89, 208, 229
primary 44, 47, 56, 103, 109, 145, 202, 235, 258, 259
problem 44, 205
problems 205, 216
problem statement 51, 53, 54, 86, 87, 107, 202
process 1, 3, 4, 6, 7, 11, 28, 36, 42, 44, 45, 50, 51, 52, 53, 56, 61, 65, 67, 68, 69, 100, 108, 110, 112, 113, 118, 127, 157, 168, 202, 226, 236, 275, 308
product 45, 52, 208, 210, 214, 217, 226, 227, 229, 230, 250, 313
production concept model 57
professionalism 18
profit margin 12, 13
projection 36
prototype 43, 45, 217
prototypes 45, 217
prototyping 43, 192

Q

qualitative 44
quality 3, 89, 247
quantitative 44
quantity 54
questionnaires 63
questions 204, 205, 216
quotation 154
quote 36

R

rapid prototyping 55, 217
readability 15, 20
readable 15, 19
receivables 32, 163
recommendations 24, 61, 64, 104, 113, 239
refine 45
reframing matrix 215, 231
reimbursements 9
relationships 27, 53, 57, 204, 279
rent 13
repetition 19
reputation 3
research 210, 311, 313
resources 6, 10, 30, 48, 125, 129, 193, 204, 210, 216, 219, 229, 235, 258, 269, 272, 279
resume 15
retainer 10, 196, 197
review 3, 9, 44, 45, 64, 66, 68, 97, 129, 130, 171

Rickards, Tudor 213, 232
risk 3, 107
risks 44
royalties 178, 192, 193
royalty rates 187, 188, 193

S

Sachichi Toyoda Sakichi 202
sales 3, 5, 32, 38, 154, 163, 164, 175, 189, 190, 192, 193, 195, 214, 230, 271, 280
sans 15, 16
sans serif 15, 16
sans-serif 16
Savannah College of Art and Design 53
scale model 59
scenarios 42, 44
schedule 4, 9, 31, 46, 60, 63, 75, 81, 96, 97, 104, 120, 125, 129, 154, 155, 158, 164, 168, 169, 170, 196, 218, 240, 258, 306
scope 44
scope of work 10, 164, 165
screener 62
script 16, 63, 64
secondary research 44
segment 210, 250
segmentation 37, 49, 79, 104, 208, 209, 244, 245, 280
semantic relationships 53
serif 15, 16
service 45, 52, 208, 210, 214, 226, 227, 230, 250, 310

service design 48
services 141, 151, 153, 154, 155, 158, 161, 164, 186, 187, 196, 197, 226, 229
size 16
skills 16
smart goals 46, 219
social 211
solution 25, 33, 55, 81, 83, 88, 148, 205, 208, 213, 216, 219, 232, 239
specific 8, 28, 39, 50, 56, 59, 64, 84, 174, 177, 210, 218, 223, 236, 240, 250
stakeholder 39, 50, 67, 103, 108, 110, 202, 235
stakeholder map 202
stakeholders 44, 45, 52, 67, 204, 210, 215, 231, 235, 250
stay focused 54
stories 52, 107
story 8, 21, 24, 52, 62, 90, 159, 160, 203, 204, 241, 271
storyboard 58, 59, 107
strategic 33
strategy 15, 20, 30, 44, 46, 77, 80, 89, 90, 93, 109, 207, 214, 225, 227, 230, 235, 309
strengths 33, 37, 47, 88, 144, 227, 261, 271
structure 234
sub-contract 165
success 8, 27, 30, 46, 47, 52, 61, 62, 69, 74, 75, 84, 86,

103, 113, 138, 139, 148, 202, 236
summative testing 61, 113
surveys 63, 150, 186, 187
SWOT 227
SWOT analysis 227
synthesis 42, 53, 97, 106, 107, 128, 129
system 15
system prototype 58

T

tasks 124, 204, 207, 216
team 44, 46, 49, 51, 54, 60, 63, 68, 69, 79, 86, 87, 96, 103, 108, 129, 130, 202, 207, 209, 215, 216, 218, 231, 234, 235, 240, 244
teams 313
techniques 47, 48, 54, 103, 217
technologies 229
template 7, 3, 32, 76, 101, 211, 227, 228
term 157, 164
termination 157, 162, 164
terms 152, 153
test 45
testing 67, 69, 112
testing scripts 223
test plan 45, 61, 112, 218, 240
text 15, 16, 18, 19, 20
threats 47, 88, 90, 227
time 10, 46, 84, 85, 155, 158, 204, 209, 219, 229, 313
too many fonts 15, 16

Toyota 202
track record 10
travel 13, 39, 49, 75, 94, 123, 131, 153, 154, 169, 174, 198, 237
trust 20, 50, 52, 78
typeface 16
typography 14, 16

U

understand 205, 208, 209, 216
unmet need 6, 44, 47, 88, 106
upper case 18
usability 59, 60, 61, 63, 64, 67, 78, 102, 103, 108, 110, 112, 113, 218, 223, 224, 225, 240, 260
usability study 63
usability testing 61, 67, 112
user 3, 9, 32, 37, 43, 44, 45, 47, 48, 49, 53, 56, 59, 61, 64, 67, 68, 69, 78, 79, 81, 86, 87, 90, 91, 103, 105, 106, 107, 108, 110, 112, 148, 210, 212, 216, 224, 244, 245, 247, 250, 253, 257, 259, 267, 269, 272
user-centered 112
user experience 49, 79, 244
user feedback 45, 110
users 42, 43, 47, 48, 49, 50, 52, 53, 55, 56, 61, 62, 63, 67, 68, 79, 86, 90, 103, 105, 107, 109, 112, 113, 210, 216, 224, 244, 250, 266, 267

V

validity 165
value 10, 12, 13, 24, 27, 31, 33,
    47, 73, 74, 75, 94, 95,
    103, 144, 154, 187, 229,
    247, 278, 279, 281, 282,
    284, 306
value proposition 12, 33, 47, 94,
    95, 144, 278, 279, 281
version 34, 60, 119
vertical prototyping 56
video 227
video prototype 59
video Prototyping 43
vision 16, 44, 45, 46, 47, 52, 84,
    257, 273, 313
visual 15, 16, 19, 20, 53, 54, 57,
    58, 64, 105, 108
visual hierarchy 15, 16, 20

W

want 205, 211
weaknesses 32, 37, 47, 88,
    144, 163, 205, 227, 229,
    261, 271
web site 217
weight 15, 16
white board 227
why write proposals 2
wireframes 61
Wizard of Oz 43
workarounds 51
WWWWWH 204

Index

YOU MISS 100% OF THE SHOTS YOU DON'T TAKE

WAYNE GRETZKY
Canadian-American ice hockey player

**DCC ONLINE COURSES
BOOKS IN THIS SERIES**

DCC ONLINE COURSES
available at: http://dcc-edu.org

OUR MISSION
Through our online programs, workshops and publications we provide skills to fulfill evolving work roles and to to create better solutions in a new economy. We provide quality education which is better value, more accessible, more flexible and more relevant for working global professionals. Online live, interactive continuing education courses that you can access from home, from work or anywhere with an internet connection.

ABOUT US
Our programs are for working designers and anyone seeking design and management training. Our online programs are presented direct from Los Angeles by some of the most experienced design professionals in the world. We offer introductory courses, five-week certificate programs and eight-week advanced certificate programs that meet once per week. The courses are delivered at a number at different times to fit your schedule and time zone.
Our books have been specified as texts at many design and business schools including the University of California, Art Center Pasadena, Parsons Graduate Program, and Purdue University. We can present a custom program in your location anywhere in the world. We can tailor an online program to your schedule and needs.

WHO HAS ATTENDED OUR COURSES?
Past participants in our online programs have included thousands of executives, design managers, designers from all design disciplines, architects, researchers, social scientists, engineers and other decision-makers from the following organizations Including the following organizations. Tesla Motors, NASA, Kaleidoscope, Speckdesign, Intel, Nike, MillerCoors, Radiuspd, Gensler, Herman Miller,Trek bikes, Catalystnyc, Sylvania, Whipsaw, Berkeley University, Stanford University, Pininfarina, Inscape, Newbalance, MIT, Rhode Island School of Design,Tufts, Nokia, Steelcase, Mayo Clinic, Ocad, California State University Santa Barbara,University of Michigan,In Form, RIT,Honeywell, Columbia University,Nissan, Volkswagen, Sony, Nestle, Kraft Foods, Otterbox, Henry Ford Museum, Samsung, Ammunition, Siemens AG, Group, frog Design, Ziba Design, Plantronics, Luxion, Philips, Method, Visteon, Texas Instruments, Cisco, Mindspring, Hasbro, Dow Corning, Bressler Group, Reebok, Logitech, HP,CCS, Praxxis Design, Levi Strauss, NCSU, Design & Industry, Kensington, Symantec, Canberra University, Australian Government Department of Defence, Maya, Karten Design, Autodesk, Barco, Shutterstock, Lucid, Colgate, Starbucks, Sunbeam, Seimens.

Register for our half-day proposal writing on-line course

www.dcc-edu.org

- Online 3 hour class in writing successful product design proposals.
- Online introductory 3 hour class in Industrial Design.
- 5 class certificate programs in Industrial Design.
  One 3 hour class per week
- 8 class advanced certificate programs in Industrial Design.
  One 3 hour class per week

Email us for more information:
info@dcc-edu.org

BOOKS IN THIS SERIES
available at: http://dcc-edu.org

DESIGN THINKING

DESIGN THINKING PROCESS AND METHODS MANUAL 3RD EDITION
Author: Robert A Curedale
Published by:
Design Community College Inc.
August 21, 2016
Paperback: 690 pages
Language: English
ISBN-10: 194080549X
ISBN-13: 978-1940805498

DESIGN THINKING PROCESS & METHODS GUIDE 2ND EDITION
Author: Curedale, Robert A
Published by:
Design Community College, Inc
January 2016
Paperback: 422 pages
Language: English
ISBN-10: 1-940805-20-1
ISBN-13: 978-1-940805-20-7

DESIGN THINKING PROCESS AND METHODS MANUAL 1ST EDITION
Author: Robert A Curedale
Published by:
Design Community College Inc.
Edition 1 January 2013
Paperback: 400 pages
Language: English
ISBN-10: 0988236214
ISBN-13: 978-0-9882362-1-9

DESIGN THINKING POCKET GUIDE 2ND EDITION
Author: Curedale, Robert A
Published by:
Design Community College, Inc
Jun 01 2013
Paperback: 228 pages
Language: English
ISBN-10: 098924685X
ISBN-13: 9780989246859

DESIGN THINKING QUICK REFERENCE GUIDE
Plastic laminated
Loose leaf one page
Author: Curedale, Robert A
Published by:
Loose Leaf: 1 pages
Publisher: Design Community College Inc.; 1st edition (2015)
Language: English
ISBN-10: 194080518X
ISBN-13: 978-1940805184

DESIGN THINKING TEMPLATES & EXERCISES
Author: Curedale, Robert A
Published by:
Design Community College, Inc
2016
eBook 51 pages
Language: English
ISBN-10: 1-940805-16-3
ISBN-13: 978-1-940805-16-0

MAPPING METHODS

EXPERIENCE MAPS
JOURNEY MAPS
SERVICE BLUEPRINTS
EMPATHY MAPS
Author: Curedale, Robert
Published by:
Design Community College, Inc
March 2016
Paperback: 402 pages
ISBN-10: 194080521X
ISBN-13: 978-1940805214

SERVICE BLUEPRINTS
Author: Curedale, Robert
Published by:
Design Community College, Inc
March 2016
Paperback: 152 pages
ISBN-10: 1940805198
ISBN-13: 978-1940805191

JOURNEY MAPS
Author: Curedale, Robert
Published by:
Design Community College, Inc
March 2016
Paperback: 152 pages
Language: English
ISBN-10: 1940805228
ISBN-13: 978-1940805221

EMPATHY MAPS
Author: Curedale, Robert
Published by:
Design Community College, Inc
March 2016
Paperback: 152 pages
Language: English
ISBN-10: 1940805252
ISBN-13: 978-1940805252

AFFINITY DIAGRAMS
Author: Curedale, Robert A
Published by:
Design Community College, Inc
March 2016
Paperback: 128 pages
Language: English
ISBN-13 978-1940805269
ISBN-10 1940805269

MAPPING METHODS: FOR DESIGN AND STRATEGY
Author: Curedale, Robert A
Published by:
Design Community College, Inc
April 2013
Paperback: 136 pages
Language: English
ISBN-13 978-1940805269
ISBN-10 1940805269

SERVICE DESIGN

**SERVICE DESIGN
PROCESS & METHODS
2ND EDITION**
Author: Curedale, Robert A
Published by:
Design Community College, Inc.
Edition May 2016
Paperback: 589 pages
Language: English
ISBN-10: 1-940805-30-9
ISBN-13: 978-1-940805-30-6

**SERVICE DESIGN
250 ESSENTIAL METHODS**
Author: Curedale, Robert A
Published by:
Design Community College, Inc.
Edition 1 Aug 01 2013
Paperback: 372 pages
Language: English
ISBN-10:0989246868
ISBN-13: 9780989246866

**SERVICE DESIGN
POCKET GUIDE**
Author: Curedale, Robert A
Published by:
Design Community College, Inc.
Edition 1 Sept 01 2013
Paperback: 206 pages
Language: English
ISBN-10:0989246884
ISBN-13: 9780989246880

DESIGN METHODS

**DESIGN METHODS 1
200 WAYS TO APPLY
DESIGN THINKING**
Author: Robert A Curedale
Published by:
Design Community College Inc.
Edition 1 November 2013
Paperback: 396 pages
Language: English
ISBN-10:0988236206
ISBN-13:978-0-9882362-0-2

**DESIGN METHODS 2
200 MORE WAYS TO APPLY
DESIGN THINKING**
Author: Robert A Curedale
Published by:
Design Community College Inc.
Edition 1 January 2013
Paperback: 398 pages
Language: English
ISBN-13: 978-0988236240
ISBN-10: 0988236249

**50 SELECTED DESIGN
METHODS**
Author: Curedale, Robert A
Published by:
Design Community College, Inc.
Edition 1 Jan 17 2013
Paperback: 114 pages
Language: English
ISBN-10:0988236265
ISBN-13: 9780988236264

Books in this series   311

DESIGN RESEARCH

DESIGN RESEARCH METHODS 150 WAYS TO INFORM DESIGN
Author: Curedale, Robert A
Published by:
Design Community College, Inc.
Edition 1 January 2013
Paperback: 290 pages
Language: English
ISBN-10: 0988236257
ISBN-13: 978-0-988-2362-5-7

INTERVIEWS OBSERVATION AND FOCUS GROUPS
Author: Curedale, Robert A
Published by:
Design Community College, Inc.
Edition 1 Apr 01 2013
Paperback: 188 pages
Language: English
ISBN-10:0989246833
ISBN-13: 9780989246835

INTERVIEWS OBSERVATION AND FOCUS GROUPS
Author: Curedale, Robert A
Published by:
Design Community College, Inc.
Edition 1 Apr 01 2013
Paperback: 188 pages
Language: English
ISBN-10:0989246833
ISBN-13: 9780989246835

INNOVATION

30 GOOD WAYS TO INNOVATE
Author: Curedale, Robert A
Design Community College, Inc.
Edition 1 November 2015
Paperback: 108 pages
Language: English
ISBN-10: 1940805139
ISBN-13: 978-1940805139

DESIGN FOR CHINA

CHINA DESIGN INDEX THE ESSENTIAL DIRECTORY OF CONTACTS FOR DESIGNERS 2014
Author: Curedale, Robert A
Design Community College, Inc.
Edition 1 2014
Paperback: 384 pages
Language: English
ISBN-13: 978-1940805092
ISBN-101940805090

BRAINSTORMING

50 BRAINSTORMING METHODS
Author: Robert A Curedale
Design Community College Inc.
Edition 1 January 2013
Paperback: 184 pages
Language: English
ISBN-10: 0988236230
ISBN-13: 978-0-9882362-3-3

BRIEFING CHECKLISTS

**PRODUCT DESIGN
BRIEFING CHECKLIST**
Author: Curedale, Robert A
Published by:
Design Community College, Inc.
Edition 1 2016
Paperback: 54 pages
Language: English
ISBN-10: 1940805317
ISBN-13: 978-1940805313

**WEB DESIGN
BRIEFING CHECKLIST**
Author: Curedale, Robert A
Published by:
Design Community College, Inc.
Edition 1 2016
Paperback: 90 pages
Language: English
ISBN-10:
ISBN-13:

**FURNITURE DESIGN
BRIEFING CHECKLIST**
Author: Curedale, Robert A
Published by:
Design Community College, Inc.
Edition 1 2016
Paperback
Language: English

ABOUT THE AUTHOR

Rob Curedale was born in Australia and worked as a designer, director and educator in leading design offices in London, Sydney, Switzerland, Portugal, Los Angeles, Silicon Valley, Detroit, and Hong Kong. He designed or managed the design of over 1,000 products as a consultant and in-house design leader for the world's most respected brands. Rob has three decades experience in every aspect of product development and design research, leading design teams to achieve transformational improvements in operating and financial results. Rob's design scan be found in millions of homes and workplaces around the world and have generated billions of dollars in corporate revenues.

DESIGN PRACTICE

HP, Philips, GEC, Nokia, Sun, Apple, Canon, Motorola, Nissan, Audi VW, Disney, RTKL, Governments of the UAE, UK, Australia, Steelcase, Hon, Castelli, Hamilton Medical, Zyliss, Belkin, Gensler, Haworth, Honeywell, NEC, Hoover, Packard Bell, Dell, Black & Decker, Coleman and Harmon Kardon. Categories including furniture, healthcare, consumer electronics, sporting, housewares, military, exhibits, and packaging.

TEACHING

Rob has taught as a full time professor, adjunct professor and visiting instructor at institutions including the following: Art Center Pasadena, Art Center Europe, Yale School of Architecture, Pepperdine University, Loyola University, Cranbrook Academy of Art, Pratt, Otis, a faculty member at SCA and UTS Sydney, Chair of Product Design and Furniture Design at the College for Creative Studies in Detroit, then the largest product design school in North America, Cal State San Jose, Escola De Artes e Design in Oporto Portugal, Instituto De Artes Visuals, Design e Marketing, Lisbon, Southern Yangtze University, Jiao Tong University in Shanghai and Nanjing Arts Institute in China.

AWARDS

Products that Rob has managed the design of have been recognized with IDSA IDEA Awards, Good Design Awards UK, Australian Design Awards, and a number of best of show innovation Awards at CES Consumer Electronics Show. His designs are in the Permanent collection of the Powerhouse Design Museum. In 2013 Rob was nominated for the Advanced Australia Award. The Awards celebrate Australians living internationally who exhibit "remarkable talent, exceptional vision, and ambition." In 2015 Rob was selected with a group of leading international industrial designers to provide opening comments for the international congress of societies of industrial design conference ICSID in Korea.

www.ingramcontent.com/pod-product-compliance
Lightning Source LLC
Chambersburg PA
CBHW070751230426
43665CB00017B/2330